THE
BIG ONE

Based on a True Story

*Miracles happen when you
shoot for the sun*

MIKE KRYSIUK

with Julia Bobkoff

Quantity sales special discounts are available on quantity purchases by corporations, associations, and others. For details, contact the publisher at the address above.

Orders by U.S. trade bookstores and wholesalers. Email info@BeyondPublishing.net

The Beyond Publishing Speakers Bureau can bring authors to your live event. For more information or to book an event contact the Beyond Publishing Speakers Bureau speak@BeyondPublishing.net

The Author can be reached directly at BeyondPublishing.net

Manufactured and printed in the United States of America distributed globally by BeyondPublishing.net

BEYOND
PUBLISHING

New York | Los Angeles | London | Sydney

ISBN Hardcover: 978-1-952884-60-3

DEDICATION

To my mother, Anne, father, Frank, and sister, Maryann, whose love, support, and faith kept me alive and sustained me throughout my recovery. You never gave up on me, so I never gave up on myself.

ACKNOWLEDGMENTS

This book was a long time in the making. I had to cross many bridges to get to the time and place in which I could tell my story. On many occasions I tried to sit down and write something, but my head was overflowing with so many memories and ideas I did not know where to begin. Through the encouragement of family, friends, and people I met in my journey (the list is endless), I persisted and eventually found a writer who shared my vision for both the book and film. Working with Julia Bobkoff has been a liberating and healing process for me. No one could have understood or told my story better; she put her whole heart into this project and is both generous and gifted. We also became good friends along the way.

I would like to give a special thanks to my entire family, including aunts, uncles, and cousins who were always my support team, each in their own special way; my friends; my medical team (doctors, nurses, and therapists); my daughters who are forever my buddies; and my wife, Lori, who is my sunshine and love. Finally, this project would not have come to fruition without Julia's talent and her expert editorial team: Tom Fiffer who volunteered his living room for our meetings, put a second set of eyes on the book, and assisted with all things technical; and Stacey Freeman, our meticulous copy editor. Last, but not least, I am grateful to Michael D. Butler for getting *The Big One* into print. Seeing *The Big One* go out into the world is one of my greatest dreams finally come true. As you hold this book in your hand, know that anything is possible and miracles do happen.

CONTENTS

"Shoot for the sun in everything you do, because even if you miss, you will land among the stars, and that is a great place to be." —*Mike Krysiuk*

PROLOGUE

It was 1974, my senior year of high school, and spring baseball was about to start. I stood on the front steps in my old Mets cap, the one I always wore when I did the yard work. The big maple, blazing red in the fall, was just showing its first green leaves. I looked down at my mother's prized flower beds alive with buds. Everything was changing. I took a deep breath. The wind off the Saugatuck smelled fresh and promising. *I should go fishing, maybe grab a buddy. But right now, I've got to get these chores done.*

I headed to the garage. My father wanted me to cut the grass, so I changed the oil and filled the gas tank of the old Sears mower. Luckily, I only had to change the oil once a year. I wheeled it out and fired it up. I was an outdoorsman—keeper of the yard—and my parents depended on me to maintain order. I was in my domain.

As I mowed a path across the yard, I smiled at my Aunt Frances driving by in her station wagon. She lived right next door. A few of my aunts, uncles, and cousins lived in Westport, the rest in neighboring Connecticut towns. We were a large family—a mix of Polish, Italian, Irish, and Hungarian. We had big hearts and worked hard. We always got together at weddings and anniversaries and often visited each other.

Aunt Frances was always stopping by to talk to my mom or borrow a cup of sugar. And her husband, Uncle John, one of my mother's brothers, was constantly working on some project with my dad that varied from fixing a boat motor to talking about fishing equipment or gardening— my uncle's specialty. He probably had the widest assortment of tomatoes, from cherry to beefsteak, in Westport.

As I cut a circle around the maple, I thought about baseball tryouts at Staples High and all that green grass I'd be running on soon. I was setting my goals high in my final year. I knew the competition I'd be up against, and I wanted to make that team and have my dreams come true. No more bench-warming for me! This was going to be the year of "The Big One." That was my nickname, given to me by my cousins, Johnny and Richard, when I was twelve. I towered over both of them, and it just stuck. And then it caught on at school because I was usually the biggest kid in my class, made to stand in the back row in every picture. I didn't mind. I did what the photographer wanted. I wasn't a pain in the ass. Or the kid who said, "I don't want to be in the back row anymore." I tried to keep the waters calm and just went along with the flow. My goal was to try to get along with everybody, to fit in, and never be an outsider.

In gym class I was known as a strong athlete, but when I went out for the teams, I never ended up in the limelight. Guys with one-tenth my skill always seemed to make the cut. I figured it was something to do with the parents and the Booster Club. But that happens in every story and every small town. You look for ways to get into that clique, but it's a crapshoot. And I usually ended up with the crap. I mean, I was on a first-name basis with that crap! I was usually held to the last day of tryouts and then let go. And the coach would slap me on the back and say: "Come out next year, Krysiuk."

But with this being my final year of high school, I decided it was time to set my sights higher and finally grab that brass ring. Nineteen seventy-four was going to be *my* year—no more cuts, no more playing second fiddle, no more would have beens, should have beens, or could have beens…. Like I said, this was going to be the year of The Big One! I was shooting for the sun!

And time was running out. I was now entering the final stretch of high school, and if I wanted things to change, it had to be now. I was seventeen, that age when you're never really happy with what you have, when you're always striving for something more—to be one step closer, one rung higher on the ladder. Though I was doing well at school and working as a busboy at Mario's, a popular restaurant opposite the train depot in Saugatuck, I wanted to become part of the "in crowd"— the group that always looked like they were having the most fun, the ones who always seemed to get away with everything and still come out smelling like a rose. Those effortlessly cool guys who always get the girls. It could have been the way they talked, walked, or dressed—I could never figure out how they did it. Sometimes I felt like I was a castaway in a boat on Long Island Sound—just floating off by myself. It didn't matter that I was tall and athletic, with brown hair, big blue eyes, and a good sense of humor. I even had a cool car—a green Chevy Chevelle with a quadraphonic 8-track tape player. I also had a job that made me good money and was known to play a pretty mean guitar.

On weekends, I got together with my next-door neighbor, Royce, who played drums, and we put out our own beat—improvising on songs from The Beatles, Stones, Deep Purple, Iron Butterfly, Cream, and Johnny Winter. Royce's friends would bring their girlfriends and, in turn, they would bring their friends, and sometimes we had a pretty good crowd. But if I saw a girl I was attracted to, I was guaranteed to get tongue-tied around her. Sometimes my mind would even go blank. I often thought, maybe I would be more popular if I associated with the right crowd. But I just couldn't figure out who the right crowd was. So I latched onto any group I could find that seemed right. From athletes to scholars, I shot the limit. But I wasn't considered a party type of guy. Maybe that was the problem? I liked to have fun, like everybody else, but I never overdid it. When my parents set a curfew, I stuck to it. I wouldn't step outside the lines. But this was going to be the year I changed all that. I was going to break loose, shake things up, step into the spotlight of social success and athletic glory!

But sometimes we change too fast, walk through the wrong door, or even fall out a window. In my case, probably all of the above. In one decisive moment I shifted my friends, my crowd, my personality, my work ethic, and even my attitude towards life…which ultimately nearly killed me…along with my dreams. This is the story of how I shed the chains of a follower who walked in other people's shadows and learned to shoot for the sun in everything I do, because even if you miss, you will land among the stars…and that is a great place to be.

CHAPTER ONE

After cutting the grass I put everything back in the garage and went inside to get some cold fruit punch and join my dad watching the ball game. We always sat together in the basement in front of the color TV, and he'd flip the station to channel 11 WPIX. I settled back to enjoy the game. The Yankees were shedding the ghost of their cellar dweller days, rebuilding under the new ownership of George Steinbrenner. My dad often remarked on how he completely redesigned the team from manager to batboy. The Yankees were winning again, which fired me up!

I turned to my dad. "I'm going to practice hard, lift weights, run, throw, and make the Staples team this year!"

He smiled. "And keep up in school too."

"Absolutely—the sky's the limit!"

We each had a bowl of ice cream balanced on our knee when we watched the game. I usually ate chocolate chip, and he loved chocolate fudge ripple. The basement was like our man cave. There was a pool table down there and one of those tabletop hockey games where you maneuver the players with sliding steel rods. And let's not forget the dartboard—I could always hold my own against my friends. I used to hang out down there after school with some of them—kids from the neighborhood.

My dad, Frank, wasn't the type to yell at the game. He sat calmly, eating his ice cream, and making the occasional comment on a good play or an error. My sister, Maryann, ten years my senior, stopped down a moment and grabbed a soda from the fridge.

"Who's winning?" she asked.

"Nobody," I answered, glancing at her then back at the screen, "the game just started."

Maryann looked more like my dad, with her hazel eyes and big grin. I, on the other hand, resembled my mom with the big blue eyes and a quieter disposition. My mom, Anne, was a homemaker, and my dad a stonemason. They met through mutual friends in the late '30s and often enjoyed dancing at the Maple Pavilion at Pleasure Beach in Bridgeport. That was a popular entertainment hall back then with bell towers and huge windows overlooking the water. They were such great dancers that people would stop to watch them twirling on the floor to all the big jazz hits of the era.

They came from hard-working families and were each one of seven children. My mom was the oldest and my father the oldest boy. After a whirlwind romance, they got engaged. My father enlisted, and they kept in touch through letters while he fought in the Philippines and the Battle of Guadalcanal. They were later married, my father in uniform, my mother in a simple white dress, at Assumption Church in Westport, November 4th, 1944.

At first they lived in local housing for veterans, but finally, my father bought a lot on Oak Ridge Park in Westport and began to construct a home from his own design. It was a two-story brick colonial with room for a future family, and he laid out stone-lined flower beds for my mother who loved to garden. The finishing touch was a young maple he planted in the front yard.

It wasn't long before my mother was happily cooking in her new kitchen with her very own window overlooking that beautiful tree. There she spent many years creating her fabulous dishes, many of them Polish. The house was permeated with the smells of simmering stews, casseroles, and buckwheat bread fresh out of the oven, chowders made from my father's efforts digging up clams at the local beach, and hand-rolled pierogies stuffed with cheese, potatoes, or cabbage. My family never had a frozen dinner or ingredients that weren't fresh. In the summer the majority of our produce came from my parents' sizable vegetable garden, which they tended together. One of their specialties was pickled beets, which we ate in the winter, along with other canned goods.

Before my father went to work in the morning, I used to watch him tape up his fingers to prevent them from getting shredded by rough stones and bricks. He was around 5'10" and built like a catcher, which is actually the position he played on the local teams in his younger days. He was very fast and a power hitter. Whenever we ran into his old ball playing buddies down at the marina in Veteran's Park, they would call him by his nickname, "Dynamite." Sometimes, they'd look up from fixing a boat motor and say, "I bet some of those balls you hit are still traveling!" He'd just laugh and then they would exchange family news, talk about new fishing tackle or how big their last catch was, go on about the Yankees, or gossip about friends. Sometimes they'd discuss recent headlines about Vietnam, or which local boy was in the armed forces. My dad was respected around town, known for his great masonry work and being an overall good friend to everybody. And even though his baseball days were behind him, he'd really made his mark in the local leagues.

In the 1930s, Norwalk was known as a baseball town. The New York teams—the Yankees, Dodgers, and the Giants—would come down on their days off and play in the pickup games. My dad batted many times against major league pitchers, and Dynamite always held his own. He was even scouted as a hitter by one of the New York clubs, but the economic climate of the Great Depression shifted his future. The major league stardom he might have achieved was put on the back burner because he had family responsibilities. Back then, parents and children really had to work together to survive.

My dad had a total of seven siblings and step-siblings, and as the oldest son carried a lot of the financial weight. As a bricklayer, he could not miss a single day of work because nobody was given time off back then for something like a baseball tryout. He could lose his job over it, and that would leave his family stranded. These were precarious times, and everybody was struggling. So my dad never got to find out his true potential, but this did not make him bitter. He focussed his energies on keeping his family afloat, and many of the local buildings display his artistry to this day. I still like to walk into the Norwalk town hall and look up at the ceiling and imagine him balanced on a scaffold up there, working away. I always wave to his memory.

"Enjoy the game," Maryann smiled, "I'm going upstairs to study."

Maryann was a commuter student at Central Connecticut State seeking a degree in accounting and computer science. Being very driven, she also took business courses at the University of Bridgeport and taught on the side at Norwalk High School.

My dad turned to her, "What's your mom doing?"

"Reading the paper and listening to Dr. Meltzer on the radio."

"Your mom always says he really helps people out." Then he turned back to the game. I heard Maryann's quick footsteps retreating up the stairs. I knew she'd be up in her room the rest of the night with a cup of tea, engrossed in her book. It was a typical evening in the Krysiuk household, everyone peacefully going about their own business.

Weekends also had their own kind of order to them. Saturdays were for running errands and visiting family. Sundays we all went to mass, Dad and I to the 8:15 a.m. service, my sister and mother at high noon. It was the same church where my parents were married. Like other members of the Greatest Generation, Dad never thought twice about serving his country. I don't know much about that time in his life, and the details are fuzzy, but I'm very proud of his service. My father was actually awarded the Silver Star, but he never talked about it. I wish I'd asked him more questions when I was younger, but I didn't know the importance of the honor or what to ask. He put the medal in a box and kept it in his desk drawer for years. I didn't even know it was there, or that he had many others, until years later when my sister told me about it.

She didn't know that much either, except that he was proud of his time in the Army and served as some kind of rescuer. Whenever there was a difficult mission, they'd always send my father in to get people out. He was quick on his feet, intuitive by nature, and both calm and effective under pressure. He was a scout and a gunner and could procure supplies that no one else could find. As a result, the Army had him constantly on the move. He didn't share too many stories, but he saved many men and women, even when the odds were heavily stacked against him.

Upon his return to the States, the Army sent him to Northampton, Massachusetts, to aid in the psych ward of the Northampton Veterans Administration Hospital. Though he never experienced what we now call post-traumatic stress disorder or PTSD, he found himself helping those who suffered from combat stress. On weekends he would travel home to his mom's house in Norwalk to get a breather. He told her the job really beat him up, all those patients reliving the war. He felt for every single one of them. During his time in Massachusetts, he discovered he possessed a strong gift for helping soldiers recover from their psychological wounds, and this type of work became part of the fabric of his life. Over the years he helped many veterans recover, as well as his two brothers, a niece's husband, and a cousin who suffered from PTSD after serving in Vietnam.

But when it came to talking about his own experiences in the Pacific Theatre, he said very little. My father was, by nature, a quiet guy. Just don't get him mad. He had a long fuse, but you could tell it was burning by the tone of his voice, which got louder and louder until he blew the wax right out of your ears. But it took a lot for that to happen. He was the balance in other peoples' lives, and all the skills he acquired from the war, and afterward helping veterans, prepared him well to help save and guide me when I needed him most during the darkest period of my life. Without his leadership and faith, as well as the support of my family, I don't believe I would be here.

But on a sunny day after mass, heading with my dad out to the local baseball field to throw and catch, bad times were the furthest thing from our minds. He was my personal coach and believed in my pitching potential. He always brought a bag of balls, and I carried the gloves and my favorite bat. It was a Louisville Slugger—Al Kaline model. He was an outfielder and a great hitter for the Detroit Tigers. My bat was thirty-two inches long, a perfect weight, and the ball just popped right off it. We'd spend a few hours out there most Sundays, pitching and hitting. Time just flew by.

Since I was eight, my dad taught me the fundamentals of baseball, with a focus on pitching. As I got older, his confidence in me grew. By the time I hit high school his teaching had really paid off. I was known for my sinker, which would drive the batters crazy and frustrate the umpires who couldn't always tell if it was a strike from the way it crossed the plate. When the ball came up to the batter it seemed to drop off the table, sinking so fast it caused them to swing and miss or get called on a third strike. That pitch was a "true sinker"—my favorite! And when it came to hitting, my dad gave me so much batting practice and so many special tips I was able to contact most pitches and develop my own power swing. But when I got into high school, I concentrated mostly on pitching because that's where my father and I felt I had the most potential for making the team.

At seventeen life was pretty grand. I loved spending time with my dad, especially watching the games and studying the different pitchers so I could apply their techniques to my own and discover new ways to outsmart each hitter. Baseball was my life, and I also wanted to use it as a way to become popular and attract the girls. Doesn't everybody?

As we shut off the TV and headed up to bed, all I could think about was tryouts. I lay in the dark, imagining standing on the mound, body relaxed, mind focussed, my left cleat kicking up for momentum, then leaning in a fluid motion toward home plate, releasing the ball in a perfect line toward my target, as my right foot finished forward, leaving me in a ready position to field any ball that flew in my direction. Strike three! Perfect pitch! Let the party begin!

CHAPTER TWO

The next morning, as I swung into the school parking lot, humming along with the guitar solo to "Sunshine of Your Love," I saw Susan pull into the space next to me. Now I felt extra lucky. I was not only trying out for the varsity baseball team later that day but maybe able to score a few points with Susan by telling her about it. Being on the varsity baseball team was an honor. Susan worked at Mario's with me, along with some of my buddies. I barely talked to her at work because I'd get so tongue-tied staring into her blue eyes as she tossed those salads. I'd say to my friend Ted, also a busboy, "What I wouldn't do to be a tomato in *her* salad." He'd just laugh and shrug it off.

Ted was the kind of guy who seemed to have everything—the car, the girl, the clothes, the money. His father insisted he work for pocket money, but other than that, he had everything he needed. Nothing seemed to bother him or tie him down. He never worried about missing one or two morning classes. He'd stop off for breakfast first at one of the local eateries. His friends would join him there: Jim, David, Barrett, and Brian. This was the "cool" group I was determined to become part of.

Ted was the ringleader, a James Dean type, but with dark hair. His father owned a big house on the hill in town, and he had a tennis court in the backyard. It looked like a country club. His dad even put down this new kind of foam floor for the outdoor courts. It was great for playing basketball too. Sometimes I got invited for pickup games. That's really how I got to know him. While I was making sure I was on time for school, he was probably eating with his buddies at the local diner.

Susan got out of her car and slung her purse over one shoulder then grabbed a few books.

I took that moment to snag my book bag, slam the door quickly, then turn to her and say, "Hi Susan, how are you doing?"

She looked at me over her chemistry book and smiled, "Oh, hi Mike, I got to run to class. I'm late. You going to be around at lunchtime?"

As I said, "One o'clock…" my tongue swelled from shyness, and I wondered if she heard me mutter under my breath as she walked away, "I'm going to finish my sentence one of these days." I really couldn't help it around her—she had these mesmerizing eyes, an infectious smile, and long, blonde hair like Marcia from the Brady Bunch. She also had a lot of male friends, and I was just trying to get noticed. Maybe if I were more like Ted and his gang, she would have waited for me, even risked being late?

I'd been trying to break into their group for a while. Just as I made it to the door before the bell rang, I saw Ted in his brown GT6 and the rest of the gang following behind in Dave's mother's blue station wagon. They pulled into the parking lot. Ted honked the car and slowed down beside me.

He rolled his window down. "Hey Mike, wait up."

"C'mon, I don't want to be late, haul your ass over here." I glanced down at my watch. I only had two minutes before the bell rang. I watched them park quickly and pile out of their cars. Jim led the way. Even though he was short, the girls were crazy about him. He had blonde hair, always looked clean-cut, and wore his blue football jacket. Jim was a top running back who achieved his dream of being a starter for the varsity team. He had a superior attitude; you just knew nobody was going to mess with him.

Behind him was Dave, over six feet but not quite as tall as me. He had a Beatles haircut and even though he lifted weights and was a strong pickup player in football, basketball, and hockey, wasn't that popular with the girls. I guess he was the strong silent type, with a John Wayne persona, but more into hanging with the guys than chasing girls. He was everybody's friend—male and female. You could depend on him. If you needed a hand fixing something or were drawn into a fight, he'd be there for you.

Barrett waited for Ted to get out of the car. He was his next-door neighbor and dedicated wingman. Barrett was as tall as Jim but more mild-mannered. He didn't participate in any of the school sports, but he'd always be part of the team if you needed someone in a pickup football or basketball game. He had a consistent outside shot and made a couple of game-winning plays on Ted's outdoor court that we still talked about. But he was also the guy Jim and Ted would always pick on. If something went wrong, Barrett would ultimately get the blame. But when the smoke cleared we were all good friends.

Brian suddenly pulled into the parking lot in his mom's '66 tan Rambler station wagon. He ran out to join us just as the bell rang. Brian and I had been friends since elementary school. We used to play on the same little league team—the Yankees—which was managed by my dad. And Brian was also a senior like me. The rest of the guys were juniors. We'd always been close, going through the trenches of school together from first grade through twelfth. We had a lot of good times growing up, fishing and waterskiing on the Saugatuck, and we'd always go out Friday nights of my junior year driving around trying to find where the party was at.

So, that was Ted's crowd, and all I wanted to do was be a part of it. I met Ted through Brian. Brian worked with Ted at a newly opened business called Jack Horner's Pie Shop. They had great custard pie, not to mention pumpkin. I never had to pay for it. Brian just handed me a slice, hot out of the oven. And that's how I met Ted. He was washing dishes in the back, but when he heard us talking about baseball and girls, he came out, wiping his hands on his apron. Between bites, I said, "I'm going to be trying out for pitching this year and just hope I don't have to kiss the coach's ass to play."

Brian laughed, and Ted made kissing noises and said, "Pucker up!"

After that I was invited into their group of friends, and it just started to blossom—like a dream come true. That was the summer before my senior year—when I first met Ted and was invited to the pickup basketball games on his father's modernized turf. I was the center, and we each respected each other's skill; nothing was taken for granted. I started to feel like I belonged. It was a great feeling—like that moment in baseball when you hit the winning home run in the bottom of the ninth and you watch the ball sail over the fence. For that one moment it's like the clouds part, and you see that pot of gold at the end of the rainbow. But in youth expectations sometimes lead us to discover that the pot is often empty.

On that spring morning, though, as we entered the double doors of the school, everything felt right. I was on my way to being accepted by the popular crowd, and life was changing like a 100 mph fastball striking out the big hitter. As I found myself walking down the hall with Ted's gang, girls smiling at me, I finally felt part of a winning team. And the clincher was seeing Susan look directly at me as I walked by and give me a flirty smile. Finally—me and the boys!

But was this the right team for me? All I knew was that the girls were noticing me for the first time, and the dial had shot up on my popularity meter. But as I headed into Kaplan's economics class, I felt the rain clouds set in. Or worse, the hurricane of Kaplan roll in. He was standing at the board in his studious glasses. He didn't have to say anything for us all to know to sit down fast and get ready for the class. He knew how to intimidate us with just a look. I slid into my seat, confident I had all my work done. *Bring it on*! I thought, *Let the crucifixion called "economics" begin*! As I pulled out my homework, I thought of Susan again and resolved to do whatever it took to keep proving to Ted and the others that I was the guy who fit in with their group—they hadn't made a mistake after all—I was The Big One!

CHAPTER THREE

After school, I went to my gym locker to get my sweats for tryouts. I was pumped, ready to show Coach Kelly I was prepared to be a starter for his team. First, let me tell you a little something about Coach. We didn't always get along so well. Last year I made the team as a pitcher, and I would have gladly started the games or come in as a relief pitcher, but instead, I spent all my time warming the bench getting splinters in my ass...well, except this one time. We were playing New Canaan High, and we were losing 12–3.

Coach looked down the bench in my direction and shouted, "Krysiuk—warm up! You're going in to pitch."

I grabbed my glove and went off to the side to loosen up my arm with one of the other players. I was so pumped! My arm felt great—like I could win the world series. All of a sudden Coach yells, "Time out!" I watched him stride out to the mound. He took the ball from the pitcher and motioned for me to come in: "Krysiuk! Get in here!"

I jogged out to the mound. It was a perfect, sunny afternoon in May, and the bleachers were loaded with parents, students, and teachers. But I wasn't nervous. Just psyched to show everyone what I could do. The bases were loaded, and there was one out in the bottom of the fifth.

It didn't take me long to strike out the next two batters to end the inning. I pitched the rest of the game and held New Canaan scoreless—and we almost came back to win. But one of Coach's brown-nosers struck out with the bases loaded in the last inning, and we lost 12–11. I thought I did great, but Coach didn't say boo to me. As the story goes, we lost the next two games. I mean, we got *slaughtered*. I wasn't even thought of by Coach to go in to pitch. I just sat on the bench collecting splinters again. So, that's when I decided to go in and talk to him the next morning. And that's when all hell broke loose.

I waited until there was no one else in Coach's office so I could have a private talk. I also brought Dave along as my support team. He stood outside the door, listening in. As I walked past him, he said, "Go get 'em, La Craze!" That was his personal nickname bestowed upon me in grade school. I got caught up in a lot of shenanigans with him, from pulling pranks to doing our famous cannonballs off the dock and getting the people in passing boats wet. Coach was sitting at his desk reading the paper when I walked in.

I went right up to him, cleared my throat, and said, "Excuse me, Coach, you got a minute?"

He slowly looked up and gave me a serious, no smiles stare. I continued: "Since I pitched well that last time out, I thought I would see more action. We got killed our last two games. And I feel I could do more for the team than sitting on the bench." He glowered at me, then dropped his paper on the desk, raised his arm, and pointed at the door.

"Get out of here! And don't worry about playing. Just be happy that you are on the team."

I turned around, and as I headed out, Dave, my "support," fell on the floor in the doorway, laughing his ass off. The coach followed me out, slamming the door in my face as I helped Dave get up. And that is how I ended last year's baseball season.

But I was ready for this year. I'd been lifting weights and running on the track at school. And, of course, practicing my pitching with my dad. He had me sharpen up on my curveball, knuckleball, fastball, and changeup. And I was psyched to use my famous sinker and all the skills my dad had taught me over the years. Above all, I wanted to prove to Coach Kelly—beyond a shadow of a doubt—that I was a valuable player; he could depend on me to get the job done.

As I ran onto the field to take a position, I passed him, standing there in his Staples baseball jacket, a yellow legal pad in one hand. He shot me a smile and said, "Warm up, Krysiuk! You'll be pitching soon."

As those unbelievable words fell from his lips, I felt the slate being wiped clean between us. After he'd slammed the door in my face last year, it took a while for the tension to lift. I just let it go, and it seemed he eventually did, too. But these words, as I ran past him, were pretty unexpected. Was Coach actually taking an interest in me? Had he possibly seen me lifting weights and running on the high school track? I felt more determined than ever to show him that I was the one—The Big One—his ace in the hole.

After I warmed up with the other pitchers, we each faced four batters and got into our rhythm. Coach stood behind the mound watching each one of us, taking notes on his pad. When it was my turn I just zeroed in on my mission: to make the team. When I was done with my fourth batter, he did the usual, showed no emotion, and said in his flat, business-like tone: "Thank you. Good job. Next up," then waved for the next pitcher.

Over the next two days of tryouts it was the same format: me doing all I could to get noticed by Coach and hoping all that scribbling on his pad meant something good for me. But every coach has his favorite. This year it was Jeff. He could do no wrong. He was a senior, like me, and of course his parents were part of the Boosters Club, which gave money to team sports. I will say no more. You know the rest of the story.

Jeff hung out with the Yuppie crowd and had his own following, sort of like Ted but a different flavor, more old money, kind of arrogant. It seemed his future was already set—Ivy League, the full Megillah. We greeted each other in passing, but that was about it, no emotion really. The only reason we were called teammates was because we were on the Wreckers.

The most peculiar thing was that on the last day of tryouts, Jeff turned to me as we were heading back to the locker room to shower and go home, and said, "Good luck, Mike. I hope you make the team." I was shocked. He even called me by my first name. We heard Coach yelling after us: "The team list will be posted tomorrow morning on the bulletin board outside my office."

I didn't get much sleep that night. The first thing I did when I got to school the next morning was go by Coach's office to see if my name was on the list. There was already a small crowd circling the board. Some of the guys were walking away swearing, while others had big smiles. I waited my turn and finally pushed through. Yes! There it was! And he'd even spelled my name right. I accomplished the first step—making the varsity team. Next was to become a starting pitcher. As I headed to my classes, I was one of the guys with a big smile, high-fiving other players who'd also made it. I couldn't wait to head home after school and tell my family the great news! Dad's coaching had really paid off! All that hard work and practicing were finally getting me noticed.

CHAPTER FOUR

The next morning as I put my cereal bowl in the sink, my mom handed me my brown bag lunch and said, "Congratulations on making the team. But like your father and I said last night, stick to those studies. Don't let anything slide."

"Yeah, Mom, don't worry, I got this." I took my lunch and headed out the door. It was a warm, sunny morning, perfect for rolling the windows down and playing some tunes on the way to school. I slid into my green bucket seats and flipped my stereo on. I pushed a tape by Iron Butterfly into the slot to hear "In A Gadda Da Vida." That tune felt like my theme song—with that driving beat, I could conquer anything, be it baseball or girls!

As I headed toward school, I sang along with the lyrics: "In a gadda da vida, honey, don't you know that I'm lovin' you. In a gadda da vida, baby, don't you know that I'll always be true." I swung into the high school parking lot beating my hands on the steering wheel to the driving bass and funky guitar solo. Whenever I played with Royce, I would cut loose on that part. Some pretty girls turned their heads as my music blasted out the windows. As they smiled, I started to slow down, but a little voice inside my head said: *Don't overdo it. This is not the right time or place. Get your ass in school.*

I drove past them, parked, and grabbed my book bag out of the back. I saw Susan up ahead, walking with her best friend, Nicole.

She stopped, waved, and as I got closer, said: "Congratulations on making the team!"

I grinned. *Boy, good news travels fast.*

But as I got closer, I could only mumble a shy, "Thanks."

At that moment the guys pulled into the lot, beeping their horns to get my attention. They drove alongside us, and Ted leaned out the window of his sports car and said, "Jump in, Mike, we're going to get breakfast—my treat."

Susan looked at me, a little surprised, and then said under her breath, "You're going to skip class?" Nicole also stared at me, curious to see what I would do.

"It's only once." I smiled and got into Ted's car. Susan half-smiled back, shrugged, then turned and walked off with her friend to class.

As Ted tore out of the parking lot, he said, "Making points with the ladies today, huh?"

"Nah, just saying hello. We were talking about schoolwork, nothing important. And they were congratulating me on making the team."

"Yeah, sure. I've seen the way you look at her at Mario's. With you making the team—anything's possible."

Ted pulled up to Cristo's, a little diner on the Post Road, a favorite of the locals. Dave pulled into the slot next to us, and everyone piled out. I felt like a member of the gang, like in *West Side Story*, only we all dressed in our own way, making our individual fashion statements.

And Ted looked the coolest in his brown suede jacket and white Adidas sneakers with the black stripes.

The waitress behind the counter—the owner's wife—said, "Hello, boys! Early breakfast today?"

Ted answered for all of us, "Sure, we'll have pancakes and bacon—my treat. We're celebrating Mike making the baseball team." Now I realized he was going to pay for everyone, not just me. Boy, it's nice to be "King!"

"I was thinking about having your usual ready for you but a little bird told me to hold off—there was something special about today." And she bustled off into the kitchen.

We all sat at the counter talking about last night's game—the Yankees against the Red Sox. Ted was not much of a conversationalist. He'd only speak if you asked him questions, usually stuff about girls at school.

So, I turned to him and said: "I made the team, but where are the women? It's a package deal, right?"

He just smiled and said, "All in due time. You got to learn how to act around them first."

Ted was always talking to some popular girl at school. He was the center of attention with all the pretty ones, especially at parties. It wasn't his height—he was average, probably around 5'10", and it wasn't anything particular about his looks. He had dark, wavy hair cut similar to Mick Jagger, but you wouldn't have picked him out in a crowd. Maybe it was his striking blue eyes? They had a certain intensity—almost hypnotic, like he was staring straight through you. And his shy but powerful presence could catch anyone's attention—male or female, young or old. He was almost like a cult leader, and back at his house on the hill he held court in his bedroom, a third-floor private club designed to awe his guests, with a powerful stereo, extensive 8-track collection, posters of The Stones, The Beatles, and Los Angeles Lakers basketball star Jerry West taking a legendary jump shot, and the finishing touch—a refrigerator stocked with cold brew. His father, George, was a businessman constantly traveling, and this gave Ted the freedom to entertain friends however he wished (within reason of course).

Everybody who grew up with Ted knew that his mother died when he was around eight. His father remarried when he was a teenager, and he never got along with his stepmother. She never came up the stairs to his room, and he rarely came down. Through his father's remarriage, he had a much younger half-sister. He got along with her well…there was just that tension with his stepmother hanging over his head. I guess that's why he always enjoyed going to breakfast in the morning with his buddies, rather than eating at home. He never wanted to be at that house on the hill, unless he was upstairs in his room, hanging with his friends.

After we finished eating, it was time for us to get back to school. All these new things happening to me were a little hard to believe. Ted timed it perfectly—we got back when classes were changing so we could slip in and meld with the crowd. I realized I'd missed Kaplan's class but figured I would catch up with him tomorrow. All I could focus on was finishing the day and getting to baseball practice. Ted said, "See ya later." I gave him a nod and headed to biology—one of my favorites. I was flying high. I was finally doing the things I wanted to do. And in control of my life. Or was I?

CHAPTER FIVE

My days began to fall into a pattern—going to eat breakfast with the guys, missing more classes than attending, even sometimes heading off to work instead of back to school because that's what we all did. And it felt great being part of this team. But was this big snowball heading in the wrong direction and dragging me along with it?

Before I even found my niche with Ted and his gang, I had already set up my schedule so that my school day ended at 11:30 a.m. That way I could head off to Mario's and work the lunch shift as a busboy in the afternoon. Staples High School had a work co-op program where students received credit for working. I was a good student and didn't need that many more credits to graduate, just a few required courses. My parents were pleased that I showed the initiative to succeed and supported my afternoon work at Marios. What they didn't know was that most of my mornings were now spent at the local diner, and I was starting to fall behind. The snowball was getting bigger and bigger, heading downhill fast.

I would go off to work and even forget about classes altogether, not realizing the price I would have to pay later for this wild carelessness. But hey, I made the varsity baseball team and I was becoming popular with the foxy ladies, the ones who could cut the cake with a smile, and Ted and I were becoming good friends. I was spending more time drinking beer in his room with our buddies, so what more could I want? I figured that since I was a good student in 10th and 11th grade, I could coast to the finish line as a senior. I often made second honors, and with my solid grades and good study habits, the teachers would respect me and give me a little exception when I made up some excuse or forged a note from my mother. I used a friend on the baseball team who had good penmanship to add authenticity to these letters that detailed family emergencies or different ailments I was experiencing at the time. It even looked like my mother's signature. I thought I had everything covered, everything figured out. I'd studied my ass off those previous years and believed that would be enough to get me into Norwalk Technical College to pursue a degree in electrical engineering.

I thought this plan would never fail until the teachers contacted my counselor, Mr. King, to check out all these absences. He then called my mom and that's when the shit hit the fan! Mr. King was soft-spoken but when he was upset, you knew it. Before he became a counselor, he was a gym coach and had a tough way about him. My mom later told me he cut straight to the chase.

"Mrs. Krysiuk," his tone was grave, "I'm sorry to bother you at home, but your son has missed a lot of school and is failing all his courses." She told me she had to sit down she was so upset.

"Oh my God, what are you talking about? Mike goes to school every day."

"According to his teachers, they all received notes with your signature on them. Some even stated that Mike was sick with a bad case of gas and indigestion, or that he had to stay home and help his dad because the pipes burst in the basement and you had to repair them right away."

My mom was silent a moment, taking this all in.

Finally she said, "I never signed any notes. Mike's been in good health. And we have no emergencies in our family. I will speak to my husband tonight and we will talk to Mike and straighten this all out."

"Thank you, Mrs. Krysiuk. I'm sorry I had to bring this to your attention, but it's a very serious matter. Mike's always been a good student. I don't know why he's taken this turn for the worse with his studies. At this point he's about to fail every class and not graduate on time. And I know he loves to play baseball, but he will not be able to play on the team this year unless he straightens this out."

"Thank you, Mr. King. His father and I will give him a good talking to tonight. We will let him know the drastic position he's put himself in. He will have to buckle down and get to work and turn himself around."

I walked in the back door after my lunch shift at Mario's later that day to find a totally silent house. We always entered through the kitchen and I saw past the dining table, which was neatly set for dinner, that my father was home (must have finished up a job early) and was sitting in his favorite chair in the living room, reading the paper. As he put it down decisively, my mother appeared in the archway of the kitchen. She had a very serious look on her face—not her usual welcoming smile—and I instantly knew I'd done something wrong. The tone in her voice meant business.

"Please come in the living room and sit down with us. Your father and I need to talk to you about school."

When I heard "school," I knew the jig was up. They must have found out about my escapades. I actually felt myself about to cry. I stood there speechless. I can't remember if I was even breathing. "C'mon, Mike, sit down." I followed my mother into the living room and just stood in front of the couch, staring at them in their matching wingback chairs. I'm sure I looked like some wide-eyed, convict about to sit in the electric chair, knowing any minute they were about to flip the switch and fry me.

As my butt hit the cushion my father said, "Your mother got a call from Mr. King telling us that you missed a lot of classes, and you're failing your courses. What do you have to say to that?"

It was so quiet I could hear the clock ticking on the mantelpiece. It seemed to get louder and louder, like a time bomb ready to explode.

I finally found my voice: "I *did* miss some classes."

Before I could continue my father said, "Some? Why, what happened?"

Just like with girls I became totally tongue-tied. I cleared my throat and finally answered, "I know I made some mistakes…but I was trying to be part of the crowd. And I left school grounds and went to have breakfast with Ted and the guys. Or sometimes we'd just shoot hoops in the gym. I would just go to work afterward instead of to my classes…."

My mother cut in, "What were you thinking, Mike? We're very disappointed in you."

At that moment, my heart hit the floor and depression took over.

I cleared my throat again: "Mom, Dad, I'm sorry I lost your confidence and I hope you will forgive me. I will work hard trying to make this up. I'll talk to Mr. King tomorrow at school and each of my teachers and get this all straightened out and start working to make this problem go away."

My mom leaned forward, and I thought I saw a tear form in her eye, "Mr. King also said you cannot be on the baseball team because of your low grade point average."

My dad then jumped in: "You love baseball and you were practicing so hard to get on the team this year and you're throwing it all away."

"I already know this. Before I left school today, Mr. King called me into his office and told me that I could be throwing my baseball career away."

I sighed and shifted nervously in my seat. My parents' faces were emotionless—just a cold stare from both of them. It was way worse than the time I was eleven years old and my buddies and I got caught smashing pumpkins on "mischief night"—right before Halloween. And it was even more dramatic than when I was fourteen and cutting through a backyard with my friend Dave to get to his house. We looked over and saw his blonde neighbor—an attractive German woman about thirty-five-years-old—standing in the window naked, combing her hair. And as she turned and saw us standing there staring at her, we ran off.

When we got to his backdoor, breathless and all riled up, I said, "I'm heading home," and took off, running up the hill to my house. As I walked in the door my mother was hanging up the phone.

She had that stern voice: "Where are you coming from?"

"Dave's house."

"And where were you before that?"

"Oh, we were throwing rocks in the river."

"What about Mrs. Kraus—Dave's neighbor?"

"Oh, um…." And then my tongue got thick and I couldn't talk.

"I just got a call from Dave's mother saying Mrs. Kraus caught you two peeping in on her while she was combing her hair. And she wasn't wearing a thing. She was changing her clothes…and she's calling you two Peeping Toms! What do you have to say for yourself?"

"Mom, we were just cutting through her yard. And we saw someone looking through the window. We couldn't make out who she was. So we just kept going."

"You stopped and stared."

"No, Ma! We didn't do that."

'You go to your room. Just wait until your father gets home!"

That half-hour wait before my father arrived felt like an eternity. I didn't know what to expect. I almost started crying, just like today.

I finally heard the screen door open and slam and my father say, "Where is he?"

"In his room, waiting for you."

Waiting for what?

I heard his tired, after-work steps down the hall, and then my door opened. He shut it very quietly and sat down backward on the desk chair, facing me on the bed. We looked at each other for a moment.

And then he said: "I've heard you've had a very active afternoon. Where were you?"

"Dave and I were down at the river…."

"Yeah, but after that?" As he said this, he kept a straight face and I thought my heart had stopped.

"Dad...."

He cut me off right there. "You're fourteen, and you are going to have an interest in women. And you both have different...equipment. I heard about Mrs. Kraus. I don't know how it happened. It's part of nature. You are going to be interested in women—but don't go spying on them."

As he said that, he started to smile. When I saw that slow grin, I felt the heavens had parted, but I was still unsure what was going to happen next. The hair on the back of my neck was still standing up. My dad finished with: "We all go through these things. But do me a favor—in the future stay away from the Kraus's backyard." He stood up and squeezed my shoulder. "I'll talk to your mother. Everything will be alright. Don't worry about it, Mike."

At that moment, I felt my heart start to beat again.

But this time was far worse than my past transgressions. I was seventeen and a lot more was expected from me. I was getting lost in other peoples' shadows, trying to be the person I wasn't, instead of working towards the student and athlete I should have been. And I knew it. I was ashamed of myself for letting my parents down the way I did. Yet, I still felt this pull towards Ted and his gang that was so strong I wasn't completely sure I could ever break free of it.

But I did say to my parents: "I'm sorry you lost faith in me. I will see my teachers and get this all straightened out. And I will get back to playing baseball this year—I promise. I'm really sorry, Mom and Dad, I let you both down."

At that moment, my dad sat up in the chair and looked at me with his warm, hazel eyes that could never hide his affection: "We will never lose our faith in you, Mike. We will work with you to get you back on track. But no more crap like this."

I nodded and let out a sigh of relief.

All the noise seemed to flood back into the room. My mother stood up and smiled at me: "Let's have a good dinner—and you hit the books before you go to bed. Tomorrow you start on that road to recovery."

And that's what I planned and hoped it would turn out to be. But as I headed into the kitchen to sit down for one of my mom's "gourmet" dinners—pork chops and applesauce—I had a sinking feeling I was still not in control of my destiny.

CHAPTER SIX

When I got to school the next day, I headed straight for Mr. King's office. His door was always open. He saw me standing there, hesitating to go in.

"Come on in, Mike. Sit down." I took a seat opposite him. "I just got off the phone with your sister. She told me you spoke with your parents after I talked with them and you worked everything out. I'm happy to see you in here, first thing in the morning. I have a schedule printed out for you." He handed it to me. "I talked to all the teachers. They are very supportive of you and want to give you a second chance."

"Even Mr. Kaplan?" I'm sure I had a look of fear on my face.

"Don't worry about him. I know he's a ball buster. We talked and everything's gonna work out. You just have to make the effort." Mr. King stared at me hard for a moment.

"I will. Don't worry about that." I stood up and folded the schedule, slipping it in my bag. I was almost out the door when Mr. King called me back.

"One more thing, Mike. Is it true you hang out with Ted Reynolds and his group of friends?"

I slowly turned and looked at him hard. "Yeah, so…?" Why are you asking me?"

"I know it's, ah…tempting to hang with these guys, with everything they've got going on. But they're having a lot of trouble with school. I don't want you to fall in with the wrong crowd…and I feel this *is* the wrong crowd for you. I know it's tough to tell you this. You can't really brush them off all of a sudden. But you don't have to lose their friendship—just don't be a follower, Mike. These guys…I heard a few bad things. If they give you any pressure or anything or make you do something you don't want to do…come talk to me. Please? 'Cause I want to see you come back with your studies. And I want to see you pitch this year for the team."

"Thanks, Mr. King," was all I could muster as I tried to wrap my mind around what he was asking me to do. It made me even wonder if he'd been in my shoes once in high school, back in the dark ages when he was young.

My first day back with a new attitude went by fast. As I left Mr. King's office the morning bell rang, and I got sucked along through the hallways with everybody else. I saw Ted and the boys up ahead and pushed my way through to catch up with them. Ted turned and smiled, "What's up, Mike?"

"Today's the first day on my road to recovery."

Dave laughed, "What are you talking about, La Craze?" He still called me that, along with "Crazy Krysiuk" at times, because I was becoming more and more unpredictable, willing to take risks in my senior year for popularity. For example, when Ted wanted to buy beer I always volunteered to do it because I was so tall I could pass as an eighteen-year-old. No one ever asked for my ID, and it made me look cool to the girls. Like I said before, I was a senior, and Ted and the guys all juniors. I had more to lose but I took chances anyway. I thought I was somehow above the system—that I could never get caught or slowed down. But clearly, Mr. King was showing me otherwise.

Jim, with his football bag slung over his shoulder, now chimed in, "Recovering from what?"

"Well, right now I gotta hang that La Craze hat up indefinitely because I'm so behind in my studies I have to look down to see up."

As Barrett turned into his English class, he laughed, "Cut the crap, Krysiuk. See you guys later."

"Yeah, later, Adios." And I headed into Mr. Kaplan's economics class, deciding to sit in the front row this time, not the back, making a good impression. *Let the circus begin.*

The whole day went well, every teacher happy to see me back on track. I raised my hand, made myself answer questions I usually knew the answers to but normally chose not to say anything. Other students gave me a funny look, and one said, "Hey, the big guy can talk." I smirked, my mind focussed on my mission to get back in everyone's good graces. I could almost smell the fresh cut grass of the baseball field and hear the whoosh of the bats as I struck out my imagined opponents; my driving goal was to stay on the team and be a starting pitcher—a powerful force to be reckoned with.

As I headed out of the school after the final bell, Susan walked alongside me. Normally, I wouldn't be able to utter a word, but for some reason I heard myself say, "Hey, how are you doing?" with the perfect ease of Ted or Jim.

It worked like magic and she looked up at me and said: "Great. I heard from Ted you were hanging that La Craze hat up. What did he mean by that?"

"I'm getting my ass back in gear, my grades up, so I can play baseball this year."

"Oh, that's cool. I got to go now. I'm working the dinner shift tonight. When do you work next?"

"Two days from now— Friday night."

"I don't remember if I'm on lunch or dinner that day, but if it's dinner, I'll see ya." And with that she took off—my dream girl—- disappearing through the crowd.

Before I could even say goodbye, Ted slapped me on the shoulder. "Ahh, scoring points, huh?"

I just grinned, "Yeah, sure."

We walked together to our cars. Ted's Triumph was always shining in the sun. He went to the car wash a lot. My 70 Chevelle may not have been as appealing to the eye, but I had the tunes, and that rules in my book.

As Ted got in he rolled down the window and said, "See ya tomorrow," and then with a challenging smile, "for breakfast."

I looked at him, flipped him the bird, then got into my car. The moment I turned the key in the ignition, the radio blasted: "Born to be Wild." I rolled my window down so Ted could hear it. He flipped me the bird back and drove off, burning rubber.

CHAPTER SEVEN

My next couple of weeks became a blur of attending classes, passing tests, saving the money I made working as a busboy, practicing my pitching with my dad—he still had his mitt from when he played catcher for the Pastimes Club—lifting weights in my basement, and relaxing with my guitar. I was on track, in the groove, headed in the right direction. I was a man on a mission and wouldn't let anything stop me. I'd made mistakes, but they were in the past, and they were going to stay there.

Mr. King was so pleased with my progress he called me into his office and said, "Mike, you're still on the team, as long as you keep up the good work."

"Wow, thanks!"

"I'll see you at the first game," he reached across his desk and shook my hand. "Hopefully you'll get to pitch. I heard you have a mean sinker."

"If I get called to the mound—I'll be sure to throw one in your honor."

He laughed and patted me on the back as he ushered me out the door.

Our first game was against Norwalk. They were the best team in the league. Jeff pitched the whole game, but we lost 2-1. Their power hitter slammed a two-run homer in the ninth inning. I saw Mr. King stand up in the bleachers and slam his hat down angrily. He was as frustrated as the Wreckers.

As I helped carry the equipment back to school, I heard the coach say to Jim, "You'll get 'em next time."

Next week's game was against New Canaan—another top team. During practice, Coach told me to be ready, I might see some action. Our starting pitcher gave up six runs in the first inning. By the fourth, I was finally put in. I looked into the stands, but Mr. King hadn't made it to New Canaan that day. We were losing 8-0 at that point, but I pitched well.

"Good effort," Coach said as we walked to the bus.

"Thanks," but inside I was thinking: *why didn't you start me instead of the guy who got shelled?*

It was always easier to get encouragement from Dave, who said: "Way to go, La Craze, you almost pulled it off."

Ted threw an arm around me: "Let's go celebrate—'cause you just got a chance to show the coach your stuff...and that was some good stuff!"

"Hold it guys, I gotta play it low key. I can't go partying yet. I just saved my ass in school. My parents are on *my* side now. I have to go home, hit the books, and tell them I finally got to pitch. Plus, I still have to hand in that big project to Kaplan, or he'll kick my ass."

"Not much to kick," Dave said, raising his boot menacingly.

I twitched away, turning the motion into a crazy, sexy walk. I had spied Susan and some friends following behind us, and my silly little dance was for their benefit. I guess they liked it because the girls started to whistle and hoot.

"Nice moves, Crazy Krysiuk!" Susan called out.

I just waved at her and said, "Thank you, Madam!"

When I got home, my sister was in the kitchen eating a grilled cheese. There was even one on the table for me, cut in half just how I liked it.

"I knew you'd be hungry after the game. Come on, sit down, Mike, and let's talk. Guess what—a letter came for you today." She placed an envelope dramatically on the table. "Tadah! I've been wanting to watch you open this all afternoon."

I glanced down and saw the return address: Admissions Office, Norwalk Tech. "I'm surprised you didn't try to steam it open," I teased.

"Let's just say I thought about it." My sister laughed. Her whole face lit up when she was amused by something. I had a good feeling about this letter. I poured myself some fruit punch while she impatiently looked on, then filled a bowl with potato chips. "The suspense is killing me! C'mon, bro!"

"Drumroll please!" I said, grabbing a pair of scissors from the kitchen drawer. Maryann obliged, tapping her hands rhythmically on the counter. I sat down with my snacks and carefully slit open the envelope. I pulled out a single page. I started reading to myself. She just stared at me, waiting. I decided not to torture her any longer and read it aloud: "Mr. Michael Krysiuk, We are pleased to inform you that you've been accepted to Norwalk State Technical College for the fall 1974 semester…" I stopped right there and looked up at her. Now she was positively beaming.

"Way to go, Mike—I knew you could do it! Now you got something to work for. Just make sure you don't get distracted again."

"I know, I know, don't rub it in. Mom and dad already read me the riot act."

Just then, the two of them walked in. "Guess what?" Maryann blurted before they could even put their keys down or hang up their coats, "Mike's got some great news for you!"

My mom's eyes darted back and forth between us. "What is it? Did you get to pitch?"

"I did but this is even better. I got into Norwalk Tech. I'm going to college!" I handed the letter to my dad. He read it to himself, my mom looking over his shoulder. Then they both just stared at me with huge grins.

Finally, my dad said: "Congratulations, Mike! See—when you put your mind to something, you can do anything you want."

My mom hugged me hard, "I'm proud of you, son." And that was all the motivation I needed to go and finish that economics paper for Kaplan.

"Where are you going?" My mom called after me as I grabbed my book bag and started to head up the stairs.

"I'm going to do a good job on that last paper for Kaplan. After I hand in this ten pager on running a business, I'll be all caught up. It's due right after our next game, and the coach said he hasn't decided yet, but he's considering putting me in to pitch."

My dad called up the stairs, "When's your next game?"

"Tomorrow, that's why I got to get this done now. I won't have the energy to work on it after the game."

"Good planning!"

An hour later, Maryann appeared in my doorway with another big glass of fruit punch for me (I was addicted to that stuff, which my mom made by mixing all kinds of fruit juices and teas together).

"How you doin', bro?"

"I'm almost done. Geez, after all these profit and loss statements, stock market quotes, and tips on how to invest your profits, maybe I should skip college and just open my own business—start a lemonade stand in front of our house. And you can be my personal secretary."

She laughed and handed me the punch. "What are you going to call it?"

"The way things are going lately—Sour Mouth." I lifted up all the pages and showed them to her. "I feel like I'm writing the Declaration of Independence. I'm gonna retitle this—'The Declaration of Kaplan.'"

We both cracked up.

"I've heard about him. He's tough. Shows no emotion. You don't know what he's thinking—never know if you're coming or going. But you'll do fine, bro. You *always* do. I gotta head to bed. I got a test in the morning in my data processing class."

"Sounds like a ton of fun."

"Yeah, but if I want to teach, it's what I gotta do!"

And off she went to bed while I kept the light on until my paper was finally finished. I squinted at the clock: 1:30 a.m. The whole house was silent. I could hear the wind blowing through the maple leaves in the front yard. I shut off the lamp with a sense of victory. I swear that was the best sleep I ever had.

CHAPTER EIGHT

As I drove to school the next morning, I rolled down the windows and blasted "Frankenstein." I saw a couple of pretty heads turn as I passed down Main Street, and one old lady gave me a dirty look. But I felt great; I didn't have a care in the world. It was a sunny spring morning, and the light glinted off the Saugatuck. I slapped the steering wheel to the beat of Edgar Winter's wild synthesizer. As I swung into my spot in the high school lot, my furry dice seemed to dance in rhythm to the song.

Brian pulled up beside me a minute later in his mom's Plymouth Rambler. I quickly rolled up the window, grabbed my bookbag, and locked the door.

As we walked into school together, he said, "What are you so happy about, Mike?"

"I finally made it—finished all my catch up work—that damn economics paper I had to finish for Kaplan. I don't have him today. But I'll hand it in to him tomorrow morning. I have him second period."

"That's cool. You had a close call there."

"Yeah, I almost had to sell the shit house."

"Why?"

"Why do you think? I almost lost my ass catching up. But I just found out I got accepted to Norwalk Tech."

"Alright, man! That's cool!" He fist-bumped me.

"I'm never falling behind again. That was a long road coming back, filled with so many God damned potholes. Geez!"

School went by fast. All I could think about was the big game against New Canaan and my chance to show my skills. I was pumped and ready to go. Susan and Nicole passed me in the hall.

Susan gave me one of her cover girl smiles and said, "Good luck at the game, Mike."

My heart skipped a beat. "You gonna be there?"

"Oh yeah, I'll be there with everyone else cheering you on."

Then Nicole giggled and said, "I'll be there, too."

Jim sometimes thought Nicole had a crush on me, but I always said, "No, she's after you."

When the last bell rang, I went out to my car, threw my books in the back seat, and grabbed my mitt. The bus from New Canaan was already pulling in, so I jogged to the locker room. I knew I had to hurry because I always got my knees taped before the game.

As I sat on the trainer's table, I heard all the guys laughing and psyching themselves up in the locker room next door. It seemed like Don took forever wrapping my knees, but you got to wait for perfection. And I wanted to be in top shape for this game.

Finally, Don said: "Next." And I jumped off the table.

Twenty minutes later I was out on the field, warming up with Phil, the backup catcher. He usually played in the outfield, but I needed someone to throw with. "C'mon, let's go," I shouted to him.

"Sure, Mike."

I worked on my fastball, getting the control, not really throwing hard, just tossing to get my arm warmed up. I was saving the powerful stuff for the game. That's when I would cut loose. No point in burning the candle out before we needed it. Then Coach called everyone in. The stands were filling up now, not just students but teachers, too. As I walked to the bench, I noticed Kaplan sitting in the front row. We smiled at each other, and I tipped my cap.

Once on the bench, I thought: *Arm, don't fail me now. Let the show begin!* I took one last look at the crowd before focussing on the game. That's when I saw Ted and the gang give me a thumbs up, yelling: "Go for it, Big One!" Susan and Nicole were sitting right next to them, looking excited.

I thought: *I sure am The Big One, taller than every other guy on this bench. I stand out like a sore thumb, like putting ten pounds of dirt in a five-pound bag—just doesn't feel right. At least my height's my strength—got to intimidate those batters!* I glanced over at Jeff, tall and thin, warming up on the mound. *Thank God I'm not scrawny like him. I can really put some power into my throws.*

But I was still rooting for him, at least in the beginning of the game. Then that little devil that sits on all our shoulders started whispering in my ear: "Don't do that well, Jeff. The Big One's got to get in there, too." As the game progressed, we all saw that our star pitcher was losing his mojo, getting hammered by the best hitting team in the league. Jeff was now slapping his glove against his leg and making faces at the umpire when he wasn't getting calls in his favor. The New Canaan batters were getting base hits, and it seemed like nothing could stop them. By the fifth inning, the score was 7-1. Coach was getting all riled up and red in the face.

He paced in front of the bench, yelling at Jeff: "You want to be a benchwarmer like these flounders over here?"

I mumbled, "Thanks, Coach, don't forget the free splinters!" A few players sitting next to me heard my comment and laughed. One even gave me a thumbs up. Jeff walked the next guy, loading the bases.

"You're pitching like you're in Little League—c'mon!" The coach was furious now. I almost felt bad for Jeff. At that exact moment we all turned and saw a Met's scout, dressed in a Met's jacket, hat, and sunglasses, taking a key position in the bleachers. We all started shouting: "C'mon Jeff, C'mon!" This was his big moment. We wanted to give him some support, get his head back in the game.

I turned and saw Ted had come down from the bleachers and was leaning against the metal fence, a girl on each arm.

He caught my eye and then shouted at the coach: "Get that rag arm out of the game. Put Krysiuk in there and let him show us how it's done."

At that exact moment, I heard the bat crack and stared with everybody else as the ball flew over the centerfield fence. The New Canaan fans stood up and screamed as the batter rounded the bases.

Our coach ran onto the field yelling, "Time out!" He motioned to the umpire to toss him a new ball. Then he gave Jeff the thumbs out and pointed directly at me. I was caught off guard. I knew I was going in to pitch, but I still pointed at myself in disbelief. A couple of people laughed.

The coach shouted: "Get in here, Krysiuk."

I jumped off the bench and strutted to the mound. Coach handed me the ball and said under his breath: "Show us what you got, Mike."

As I warmed up, taking command of the mound, I glanced over at the scout. He removed his sunglasses and took a good, long look at me. Moments like this happen once in a lifetime, and I'll never forget it. I felt like I was a rookie in my first appearance at Yankee Stadium, like everything in my life had built to this one moment. I heard some shouts from the crowd: "Go get 'em, Big One." And then Susan stood up and got everyone chanting: "Big One! Big One!" Her face was flushed with excitement, and a lot of her pretty friends stood up and joined her.

As I wound up for the first pitch, I forced the noise out of my mind and focussed on everything my father had taught me. The first two batters couldn't hit my fastball. They both struck out. As the third batter warmed up at the plate I heard my dad's voice in my head: "Just be confident." I decided to use the infamous sinker on this guy. And thank God it worked like a charm. I struck him out and the Westport crowd went wild. As I returned to the bench the team was high-fiving me. The coach turned to us and said, "Grab your bats and get some runs— Krysiuk stopped the bleeding!"

We came back swiftly over the next few innings. The bottom of the ninth was the last time up for us. We were only one run behind. I was on deck to hit next. There were two outs. Runners on second and third. I was looking for my chance to get in there, get a base hit, and win the game for us. I watched the batter in front of me. The first pitch he popped up to the pitcher, who showed off doing a Willie Mays basket catch for the third out. The New Canaan crowd ran onto the field to celebrate. I just stood there, two bats in my hand, utterly discouraged. I'd missed my big chance. I turned and saw the scout talking to Jeff. Figures. I threw the bats down in frustration and went to get my glove off the bench.

Just then I heard an unfamiliar voice: "Mike, come here a minute?"

I looked around, straightened my hat, and saw the scout waving over at me. It was *him!* Talking to *me!*

I shouted back: "Yes Sir! Yes Sir!"

I jogged over, new pep in my stride, excited to see what he wanted. As I faced the scout, the coach and the other players listened in while throwing gear into the bags.

"Hi, I'm Len. Len Zanke—scouting for the Mets."

I finally found my voice and said to this slick-looking man with the notepad: "Thanks for coming to watch us. Not our finest moment out there."

He looked at me over his sunglasses, smiled, and said, "Nice sinker, son." At those three words, my heart stopped. He then added: "I'd like to come back and watch you pitch a game and swing that bat." He opened his billfold and handed me a business card. I looked at the small rectangle with the Mets logo then back up at him.

I was tongue-tied, as usual, but I managed to blurt out: "Sure thing!"

He reached out, shook my hand firmly, and finished with: "You're one to watch, kid."

"Thanks!" But the moment that word left my lips he was gone, heading towards the parking lot. I watched him get into his fancy sports car. We were all watching him. He tore out of the lot and was gone in a flash.

Then Ted came over: "What did that scout say?" "He wants to come back and see me pitch a game."

"Wow! We got some partying to do! Go shower and change." Ted's blue eyes looked super bright.

"Hey, I don't know. I promised I'd be home after the game."

Now they darkened. "Come on, Big 0ne! Tonight we celebrate at Vista. And tomorrow," he nodded toward his pretty entourage, "Girls…!"

They smiled at me, a pretty blonde and brunette, the kind you can look at but not touch.

"Did they leave their glasses at home?" I laughed, "Why are they smiling at me?"

Ted punched me in the arm: "There's gonna be a lot more of that. Better get used to it."

"I guess the old saying's right—dreams sometimes do come true." Then I grew more serious. "But I promised my mom and dad I'd be home right after the game."

Now the other guys, Barrett, Jim, Dave, and Brian, were standing behind Ted looking at me. They kept saying, "C'mon, Mike. C'mon, Big One. We'll be back soon. Don't be a pussy."

Ted always knew how to change people's minds. "Look, my car's faster. We'll leave yours here, take mine up to Vista. Be back in half an hour."

Then Dave chimed in: "C'mon, La Craze. You're the reason why we're going. Got to celebrate your lucky break."

"Alright, stop raggin'," I finally gave in. "But I'm NOT drinking. Just keeping you guys company. I calmed the waters at home, and I'm not stirring up any more trouble. I gotta hand that Kaplan paper in tomorrow, so we gotta make this quick. I'm not screwing up school in the morning."

Then Ted used his scornful, baby voice: "Don't worry, Mikey, we'll get you home before bedtime." And everybody laughed.

CHAPTER NINE

Vista was a combination liquor store and bar just over the New Canaan line on Route 123. This was a popular place because, in Connecticut, the blue laws restricted the sale of alcohol and beer to 8 p.m. In New York, you could buy it any time. After I showered and changed, it would be after eight. I ran off to the locker room and got washed up and dressed as fast as I could.

All the guys were grumbling about our loss, but I was excited to get the card from the scout. I placed it carefully in my wallet for safekeeping. I left the gym ahead of the pack and jogged across the parking lot to Ted's car. Turns out Jim wanted to ride shotgun, but I wanted the seat of honor, so Ted flipped a coin. I watched it spin in the air then land in his open palm. He shut his fingers quickly then slowly opened them again. I saw George Washington's face staring up at me.

"Heads—Mike's with me."

Jim shrugged and walked off. I folded my huge body into Ted's car, almost regretting the choice; this coupe was made for someone half my size.

The moment I got in, Ted fired it up and off we went. Dave swung out behind us in his mom's blue station wagon.

It was a cool, spring night, and we had the windows cracked. I could smell the fresh wind and everything felt perfect, at least until Ted flicked on the news. The radio announcer's voice was flat and somber: "US airpower is being limited by bad weather. And military analysts are wondering how many steps the South Vietnamese can take backward before they again stop and make a stand against the enemy advance…"

Ted voiced my thoughts: "I'm sick of the news. Let's hear some good tunes."

"Now you're talking. Put that tape on you borrowed—the one you keep saying you'll give back to me." We both laughed and he popped it in. The Rolling Stones blasted through the speakers: "I can't get no satisfaction."

Ted smiled at me: "Those days are over for you, buddy. After today, this song is old news."

It only took us thirty minutes to get to Vista. We swung into the busy parking lot in front of the old liquor store. Dave jumped out of his car fast, but I had to unfold my 6'4", 185-pound frame from Ted's Triumph. He handed me a wad of cash, and then I ran after Dave.

I caught up as he entered the store. Over to the right were two huge refrigerators with glass doors. There was so much beer to choose from, but we always bought Budweiser because it was the cheapest—we could get the most for our buck. I never worried that we'd get carded. Dave and I were the tallest and looked like we were eighteen.

I turned to him and said under my breath, "Just be cool like we're not stealing anything."

He winked back at me, "Ah, La Craze."

The man behind the counter had tattoos on his forearms and wore glasses. He was partially balding and well-built, maybe five-six or seven.

He just looked up at us, not too intimidating: "Is that all you want, guys?"

"Yeah," said Dave nonchalantly.

I handed the clerk the money, and he gave us the change. It was that easy. We walked out, a six-pack in each hand, ready to divvy up the beer. For a moment I stopped in my tracks, watching a pretty blonde walk by.

Then Jim reached over from the passenger seat and honked the horn at me, yelling out the window: "Get your asses over here with those Buds!" Then he honked again, showing he meant business.

Ted yelled out his window: "Stop beeping the horn. Someone will call the cops. You're making so much God damn noise. "

Then Barrett, as if he hadn't heard a word Ted just said, stuck his head out the window and stated the obvious: "Yeah, yeah, they got the beer, they got the beer!"

As I got closer, I could see Barrett through the window excitedly beating the headrest in front of him like an Indian with his war drums.

He almost hit Jim in the back of the head, and he spun around and shouted in Barrett's face: "Watch what you're hitting, boy! 'Cause if you hit me I'll knock you on your ass."

Barrett wasn't very tall, so I could picture that happening. Everybody was always beating on Barrett.

Then Dave, the voice of reason, tried to take control: "You guys are crazy. Put a lid on it. We gotta get home. We got school tomorrow and Mike shouldn't even be here."

"Yeah, I don't want to get his old man mad." Jim reached out to take the beer through the window.

I handed one of my six-packs to him. Everyone snapped one off and began to pop the tops. I leaned in the window: "See you guys tomorrow at school. Let us lead the way. I gotta get home first."

Brian toasted me from the back seat: "To the Big One! You really kicked ass today."

"Thanks, buddy! See you tomorrow."

Then I went over to Ted and handed our six-pack through his window. "Here, take it."

"Where's my change?"

"Dave's got it."

"Kiss that goodbye."

Then I folded my body back into the passenger seat. I was tempted for a moment to grab a beer then decided against it. I didn't need my mom smelling alcohol on my breath when I got home. The last time that happened she grounded me for a week. Ted popped his lid and then pushed the tape back in. Dr. John's "Right Place, Wrong Time" came on as we peeled out of the parking lot. I turned and looked through the back window. Dave's car had done its usual—failing to start. I bet he was cursing the engine. I could imagine him now: "Goddamn it, what did my old man do to it this time?"

We were far ahead of them. I sat back and enjoyed the ride. When the song got to the instrumental, I played some mean air guitar. Ted picked up speed and the telephone poles started to whiz by. It made me think of those lyrics from *Hot Rod Lincoln*: "Now the boys all thought I'd lost my sense, And telephone poles looked like a picket fence." It was a cool, clear night—no traffic on the road. The telephone poles were turning to a blur. I glanced over at the speedometer. Ted was pushing 100 mph.

I yelled at him: "Slow this goddamned thing down!"

He just laughed as the needle edged higher. The car started to shimmy. "Stop laughing you asshole—you're gonna get us killed!"

But like the Joker in some episode of Batman, he kept laughing his maniacal laugh and the car shook like crazy. Ted tried to downshift, and his face turned white. There were a lot of crunches as the gears locked. I didn't have time to panic. Ted hit the brakes hard, and they locked, too. All I could hear were these screeching tires. And then the world began to spin. I yelled in my head: *Shit! Oh my God!* as I instinctively put my feet up on the dash to brace myself. The music was still blasting. I heard the lines: "I been on the right road, but I must have used the wrong car," as I wrapped my arms around my legs and gritted my teeth so hard you'd need a crowbar to pry them open. I dug my chin into my knees and tried to make my huge body as small and compact as possible as we began to spin off the road and head towards a huge pile of dirt and a big black shadow.

The shadow grew bigger and bigger, now the size of a large tree. I squeezed my eyes shut, preparing for impact. My last thoughts were: *Why me? Why now?* Accompanied by a sense of total disbelief. And a burning desire to get out of this place, this car, this moment. I wished I was home. I wished I'd listened to that voice inside my head that told me this was the wrong choice…but I had to be one of the goddamned boys. I guess I'll never learn…

Everything shifted into slow motion as Ted's car lifted into the air. I felt like I was floating. Airborne. I didn't know what was going to happen next. I hoped if we had to land it would be on something soft. But I knew with sudden clarity that we were going to hit hard. Very hard.

At that moment everything switched into hyper speed. The front of the car flipped into the big, black shadow, which I saw, for a split second, was a bulldozer. And they don't move. Simultaneously, I felt my face explode. And I heard a deafening boom like the dropping of the atom bomb on Hiroshima. With a rending noise, the engine broke through the glove compartment. I watched it slide under my legs and slam into the base of my seat. The thought hit me—if my legs hadn't been up on the dash, I would have lost them both at the sockets.

I was still curled in a tight ball as my head struck the roof of the car. Another boom and I was instantly launched into Never Never Land. I didn't know where I was. Everything that happened after this I learned about later, like my face exploding from the rearview mirror slicing it in half. It was like being struck by an axe murderer. The jagged metal cut me from the top of my forehead, straight down between my eyes, across my left cheek, and finally flew off to the side, severing my ear into three dangling pieces. That's when my brain short-circuited and went black, like a switchboard with the power cut—all the flashing thoughts gone silent. I was instantly transported into a state of total peace. It was as if I no longer existed in the normal plane of reality. I did not hear Ted's urgent cry: "Mike…! Big One…!" I did not know that he worked to release himself from his belt and was sitting on the ceiling of the upturned car as if it were a floor, trying to communicate with me until he passed out.

I was in some other world and could not understand or define what was happening to me. I had never been like this before, not even in a dream. I didn't know what to expect or where I was heading. It was as if I had entered another dimension or reality. All I wanted to do was find out where the hell I was and how to get back. I still somehow knew I had to get to school in the morning and hand that paper in to Kaplan. But I was just floating in the ether, like a balloon tethered by its string, somehow outside my body, yet still connected. I can't explain it fully. There are no words in the English language for this bizarre sensation—at least I don't know of any. All I wanted was to get back to my family and reap the unlimited rewards available to those who right their path—a dream I'd worked so hard for—that brass ring of success that finally seemed within reach. But I was drifting between one world and the next, stuck in some in-between place that made no sense. And all I wanted was to go back home.

CHAPTER TEN

At this point, I have to go by the accounts of others, like Dave and my friends, and police reports. Dave swerved off the road and parked hard. The boys jumped out and ran towards Ted's car, which was impaled on the plow, its wheels still spinning. They could see me through the fractured windows, hanging upside down, still secured by my seatbelt. Ted remained unconscious, unbuckled, and propped up against the back of his seat. In that moment, they all thought we were dead. "Right Place, Wrong Time" ran its final riff as the wheels slowed to a stop. The last phrase hung in the air: "Refried confusion is making itself clear. Wonder which way do I go to get on out of here…." Then the tape clicked off. Nothing but the sound of cicadas. And the tension of teenage fear. Four boys just standing there, staring at the wreckage—frozen—not sure what to do.

Then a patrol car's lights swung across the field, illuminating the interior of Ted's car. Jim told me they could see everything lit up, like some set in a gruesome film: my face looked like one of those pumpkins we used to smash on Mischief Night. And Ted's gashed forehead dripped blood.

"Look at the Big One…Holy shit! No one's moving." Barrett couldn't stop babbling.

Everyone else stood silent, struck by my feet still up on the dash, my arms wrapped around my knees, frozen in fetal position.

A state trooper roughly pushed Barrett to the side: "Out of the way, kid! All of you—move back."

The distant sirens were wailing. Within minutes the dark field was ablaze with flashing lights. Police and medics descended on the scene as my friends moved to the side. The state trooper wasn't satisfied: "That's not far enough. Move over here—we have to take care of your friends now." The boys did as they were told, waiting near Dave's car as the jaws of life were rushed in.

Jim turned to Brian and Dave. "Ditch the beers. I'm going back to check on our friends."

Barrett grabbed his arm, "But the cop..."

"I don't care. That's Ted and Mike down there." And off he went, approaching a fireman who stood a few feet back from the wreck. "Are my friends OK? Are they alive…?"

The first responder saw the fear in Jim's eyes and took a moment to answer: "Time is of the essence. We have to get them out of here and to the hospital. So please go back to your car. I know you have questions and want to help. But the best thing you can do for your friends right now is give us room to do our job. An officer will be along shortly to take your statements."

At that moment I was brought by on a stretcher. Barrett left the car and ran alongside me, shouting, "Holy shit, holy shit—The Big One's dead!"

Just as my ambulance screeched away, Ted's stretcher passed by. All four friends held their breath, looking at their ringleader, their guru, their king. In the flashing lights, his blue eyes, once so fierce and penetrating, seemed glazed over, blank, unseeing. They watched in disbelief as his battered body was shoved into the back of an ambulance and the double doors slammed shut.

Dave said, "Let's follow," and everyone moved toward his car, but the trooper intercepted them.

"No, Officer Johnson has a few more questions for you, then he's going to take you all home."

So, they just stood there instead, watching the spinning light of Ted's ambulance disappear.

Once in the ER they cut my clothes off to see what kind of shape I was in. My face was cleaned and temporarily taped, along with my ear. Stitches came later. The doctors didn't have time to worry about my broken collarbone. In fact, it was never repaired. After the medical team got me cleaned up, they gave me a tracheotomy so I could breathe and not be in danger of swallowing my tongue. To this day, I have a noticeable scar where the trach was placed.

I am sure many other things were done to me, but I wasn't really there. My body was, but my mind was detached from it, and I felt as if I had somehow shifted into neutral. My parents didn't know anything yet. And the medical records are now long gone. What I do know is that a chaplain was sent along with a police officer to my house to notify my parents, while doctors and a medical team worked frantically to save my life.

While men and women in green scrubs descended on me, my sister was standing in the kitchen, spooning stew into a bowl. She'd just returned from a late night at school and, to this day, remembers the exact meal—Kapusta and Kielbasa, one of her favorites. She'd only taken a few bites when the doorbell rang. My dad was sitting in the living room reading the sports page. "I'll get it," he said, somewhat surprised at the late hour. Maryann moved, as if by instinct, to the living room, her bowl still in her hand. My mother followed behind her.

Through the big picture window they glimpsed a police car. My father opened the door and was shocked to see a chaplain standing next to an officer. Maryann said fear struck her like a lightning bolt. She almost dropped the bowl, but my mother took it from her hand. Dad remained levelheaded—like he always did. He didn't survive Guadalcanal without developing a calm surface in times of highest stress.

"What's happened?" he said quickly, "Is it Mike?"

The officer answered first: "Mr. Krysiuk, we are here to notify you that your son was in a very serious car accident on Route 123, New Canaan Avenue."

My father stood there quietly for a moment, absorbing this information. Now the soup bowl slipped from my mother's hand, hitting the floor with a loud crack. My mother stepped right over it and ran to the door, my sister right behind.

"Please, come in," my dad ushered them into the house.

As the two officials entered the living room, my mother grabbed the chaplain's sleeve and looked up into his eyes, "Please, is my son alive?"

As she waited for his answer, she frantically searched his face. Maryann steadied her by the arm, waiting close at her side. A droplet of sweat trickled down his forehead.

"As far as we know," he cleared his throat, "your son's alive."

The officer took over at this point, cutting straight to the chase: "The car your son was riding in tonight hit a bulldozer head-on and flipped upside down. He had to be cut from the vehicle." He turned and looked at my father. "We're here to give you a ride to the Norwalk Hospital ER. We need to go immediately—there is no time to spare." His eyes flicked to the chaplain. As soon as the words left his mouth, my dad grabbed his cap and jacket and headed for the door.

The officer then turned to my mother: "You and your daughter had best stay here and say a prayer for Mike. We'll take your husband up to see him."

No one questioned this. It felt like the right choice. My family instinctively knew that my father was the one best suited to handle whatever lay ahead. Before he followed the two men out the door, he took my mother and sister's hands in his. There was a family squeeze and then he said, "I'll call from the hospital as soon as I know more." And then he was gone. My mother and sister stood at the living room window watching the squad car speed down our street, my dad sitting in the front seat, staring straight ahead.

Maryann turned and led my mother to the couch. They sat together, held hands, and began to pray. This was going to be the longest night of their lives. Maryann later told me that as they bowed their heads and started speaking to God, time seemed to stand still. The only sound in the room was the tick-tick of the clock on the mantelpiece and the beating of their own hearts.

Once in the emergency room, my father followed the officer straight to the intensive care unit. They moved through the maze of halls quickly. Finally, they came to the room where I was being treated. My dad hesitated a moment before entering. I was hidden behind a green hospital curtain. My dad could only see the shadows of the medical team moving against the fabric. Then the curtain parted and Doctor Goodman stepped out. He was a confident man in his mid-forties, prematurely gray. Before speaking to my dad, he assessed him a moment. Then he held out his hand.

"I'm Doctor Goodman."

"Frank Krysiuk."

"Before you go in there, I need to warn you that Mike was severely injured and you may not recognize your son. His face was sliced open, and he's sustained a broken collarbone…but there's no time to set the break. Right now we're in critical mode trying to save Mike's life." My father blinked under the bright lights, taking this in. "Besides the cuts and bruises, he's sustained a brain stem injury, which has severely swollen his head and will require an operation to relieve the pressure."

My dad took a deep breath: "So where does that put us?"

"Brain stem injuries impact the central nervous system. Mike's in a coma, and we can't say when or if he will ever come out."

My dad stared at the shadows again moving frantically behind the curtain, then back at the doctor. Finally, he spoke. "What are the next steps?"

"First, we need to drill two burr holes in his skull to reduce pressure on the brain."

My dad did not like the sound of this. "Are you sure that's absolutely necessary?"

"To put it in layman's terms—if we don't, Mike's brain will swell up, causing irreversible damage. So, unless you want his brain to shoot out of his ears when the pressure goes down, we don't have a choice." My father nodded. "We're taking this moment by moment—and every moment counts—so your visit must be brief."

"Yes. I understand." My father took a step forward. "But I need to know—what are Mike's chances of pulling through?"

The doctor did not sugarcoat his response. "To be honest, I don't think your son's going to live. He'll be lucky if he makes it through the night." The two men locked eyes. "But if he does make it, you need to know that Mike will never be the same young man he once was.... Do you understand me?" My father nodded again. "You've got two minutes."

Then my dad steeled himself, pushed the curtain aside, and walked in.

A team of highly skilled neurosurgeons, brain trauma experts, and critical care nurses looked up. Their scrubs were soaked in blood, eyes grim. They parted briefly, making room.

My father stood solemnly, looking down at what was left of me. I don't know what horrors he'd seen on the field of battle. I do know that he was the one often sent back into the fray to retrieve a fallen comrade whom no one else could get out. But perhaps nothing can prepare a father for what my dad saw that night.

What I do know is that he leaned over me and said in that steady, calm voice that coached me through life: "God, if you want Michael to go home to heaven—then thy will be done…But please God—if you could bring him back to us—to the boy he once was before this accident—we will be forever in your debt, Almighty Father." Then he made the sign of the cross and took a step back. At that exact moment, I went into a full-body spasm, my limbs jolting on the table. My father turned to

Dr. Goodman, his voice suddenly hopeful: "Is Mike coming out of his coma?"

"No," Dr. Goodman shook his head firmly, "this is the body's response to extreme trauma. Mike's suffered damage to the portion of the brain that connects the spinal cord to the forebrain and cerebrum, and this is what happens…."

My father crossed himself one more time, then closed the prayer. "In the name of the Father, the Son, and the Holy Ghost—be with my boy. In Jesus' name, amen."

Then he turned stiffly and followed Dr. Goodman out.

On the other side of the curtain, under the glaring lights, there was a brief and final conversation. Dr. Goodman maintained his formal manner: "Go home now, Mr. Krysiuk. There's nothing you can do here. If there are any changes, the hospital will call you. I strongly advise that you prepare your family for the worst."

CHAPTER ELEVEN

I am now going to tell you what it is like to be in a coma. The last thing I remember before the lights went out was hearing those screeching tires followed by that loud smash as we flew into the bulldozer. It felt like my face exploded on impact and suddenly everything around me was in a state of complete peace; I was just floating along as if on a tire tube, sunning myself as I drifted downriver. I didn't know where I was going or how I got there. I didn't remember what happened to me. All I knew was that I needed to get home, or I would be in big trouble.

I kept telling myself everything was all right—I'd find my way to safety. I just knew I had to get to school in the morning and hand that extra-credit work to Kaplan. Then the rest would be clear sailing to graduation. I'd be able to enjoy the last few weeks of high school before I put on that cap and gown.

Those were my last, somewhat logical thoughts. My mind was losing its thread, and everything felt more and more like a dream I could not explain. I remember reading somewhere that dreams do sometimes come true—even the bad ones. At this moment, my life-changing journey began. A journey I wouldn't wish upon anyone.

Being in a coma is very confusing. My thoughts shifted like changing channels on a TV set. People, places, and things started popping in and out of my mind like some crazy slide show. I saw my car still parked in the school lot. *Hey, maybe if I took my car that night up to Vista instead of riding with Ted, this would never have happened....Maybe I never should have gone in the first place? There are so many variables to choose from; where do I start?*

People and places started racing through my mind. I saw myself as if I were watching a film, age twelve, playing on the all-star little league team. I was sitting in the dugout. I saw the back of my shirt—number fifteen—benched as always, waiting for my big break, to show my stuff. I could hear my thoughts: *Just put me in the game, come on, Coach!* Even as I was cheering for the team, I was wishing to get in the game any way I could because that dream of being a major league pitcher was burning inside me. Then the channel switched so fast that I could barely catch my breath.

I was reliving parties: birthdays, family weddings, Christmases, my parents' anniversaries, and even some high school dances. I saw myself blow out candles, a wedding bouquet sail through the air, Christmas lights shining in storefront windows as I walked down the street, going out for lobster dinners with my parents and sister, and dancing to that wild beat in the high school cafeteria, "In-A-Gadda-Da-Vida" by Iron Butterfly. I saw girls spinning in skirts like Broadway dancers. My thoughts never really settled on one particular image. They were rapidly cutting together like a flipbook, the faster the pages of my mind turned, the quicker the film moved. The past felt real—animated—like I was both seeing and reliving my life at the same time. A little here and a little there now blended together and jumping around in time.

The channel flipped again, and I saw myself walking with the boys to breakfast instead of going to morning classes at school. *We were never going to get caught because we were way too smart.* That was my thought as I opened the diner door and took a stool at the counter. It was so vivid that I could see the butter sliding across the pancake as I poured the maple syrup on. Then the cards flipped again and I was buying my first car, a 1970 Chevy Chevelle—my "chariot." As we closed the deal, my dad handed me the keys and said, "You take it home. I'll be the passenger." When I pulled onto the road, the flipbook slowed, and it felt like all the cars were parting to let my chariot through to victory. The light was bright and the sky clear blue.

All of a sudden, I was now riding in a boat. I'm not sure why I was there, maybe either fishing or water-skiing, but there I was on the high seas. It was a thirteen-foot fiberglass boat, and I was with a friend— Brian. Oh, wait a minute, that's right, we were fishing off the point at Compo Beach. I could see myself casting my shiny lure out into the water, hoping to hook some huge fish or a bathing beauty swimming not far off. Oh well, you can only hope!

Next, I was on my first date. I was sitting next to Debbie. She had long black hair parted in the middle and wide-set green eyes. I was nervous. I could hear my thoughts again: *why did she accept a date with me?* We were watching "Butch Cassidy and the Sundance Kid." When Robert Redford shot his gun, she grabbed my arm and put her head on my shoulder. Her hair smelled like strawberries. I could not believe this was happening to me. As the scene shifted to Paul Newman, I turned toward Debbie, and she gave me my first kiss. When our lips met, those damn fireworks went off in my head. I was popping like my popcorn and it fell on the floor.

The scene faded. Everything went blank as if the film ran right out of the projector. I started to feel confused, worried, even scared. I'm not sure why I felt this way. It's just that so much was happening so fast, memory after memory…I was looking for those two words at the conclusion of the film—"The End"—but all I got was a blank screen. In a coma, time means absolutely nothing. It's kind of like falling dominos, one right after the other, one scene hitting the next until your mind goes blank. At least, that's how it was for me.

Yet, I could still hear my mom and dad talking. I could recognize their voices, but I couldn't make out exactly what they were saying. It was all just a low mumble, but at least I could tell they were there. I wanted to reach out and touch them and let them know I was right here and everything was going to be OK. But I couldn't. I tried, but nothing worked. I kept telling myself to wake up. *Get moving! You have places to go, people to see!* But my body wouldn't listen. There was clearly a major break in the flow of my internal communication.

I suddenly realized something was very wrong. Too many strange things were happening in too short a frame of time. My mind could still operate, but my body had jumped the track like some cannon-balling train, severing all connections to the conductor. I guess one might say my body was dead—that the train was so far from the track, it might never get back. *I am in a coma! I am trapped in here, and I want to get out. Please, GOD! Please get me well. I want to live and walk again. Please Gooood……..!*

CHAPTER TWELVE

While I remained in my coma, my dad came home. My mom and sister were sitting at the kitchen table when he walked in the back door. They searched his face for the report before he even spoke. This was the most disturbed he'd ever looked. He sat at the table and grabbed my mom and Maryann's hands.

"Mike's in very bad shape. I'm not going to go into the specifics, but he has a brain stem injury. His body is going through traumatic shock. The doctors are doing everything they can to save him." They all started to cry. My sister told me years later that this grim news marked the most heart-wrenching and emotional moment of her life. Then my father directed everyone's thoughts to the positive. "Let's not forget—Mike had a physical for baseball just the other day, and the doctor said he's in excellent health. At seventeen, he has youth on his side. He went into this in peak condition, and he *will* recover." Then he led everyone in prayer.

After they finished bowing their heads and holding hands, my mother's thoughts turned to the earlier part of the day: "Mike should never have left in that tiny car. If I had my way, I would have told him to stay home."

"It's too late now," my father pulled her into an embrace.

Maryann gave them a moment and stood up to clear the coffee mugs and put them in the sink.

Then she turned back to my parents: "Why does Mike have to be friends with everyone—be part of the "in" crowd?" She stood there, hands on hips, frustrated. "I wish he wouldn't walk in other peoples' shadows. He's stronger than that!" Tears welled up in her eyes.

My father put a comforting arm around her. "We have to focus on the present right now. We're the Krysiuk team," his voice was firm but soothing, "And we're going to bring Mike back. All of us. Together." He looked from my sister to my mother, then back again. My mother's bright blue eyes seemed to darken with the intensity of her emotions. My father took her hand in his again. " The best thing to do is get some sleep, so we're all strong in the morning to help Mike through this battle. That's our job—to carry him through."

At that moment, my family united in spirit. My dad led the way, and everyone became focussed on the singular goal of bringing me home. Though the doctors predicted I would not make it through the night, I was still there in the morning, fighting for my life. When my mom woke up, she decided to take her crucifix with her to the hospital and put it by my bed.

When she walked in and saw me, head shaved and bandaged, a tracheotomy, my body hooked to machines and IVs, monitors beeping, her eyes filled with tears. When she leaned over my bed to kiss me, I felt them hit my face. I wished I could tell her—*I'm here, Mom, I just need help to get back to you*—but I couldn't respond in any form. At that moment, she placed her crucifix on my bedside table.

Then she took my limp hand in hers and said, "Mike--we're all here for you, praying for your quick return--for that time when you come back to us." She gave my hand a little squeeze, "C'mon, Big One—we all love and need you."

She must have stepped back then because I heard Maryann speaking close to my ear: "Hi Bro, we're right here with you. Everybody says hello, Uncle John, Uncle Nick, Uncle Joe, Uncle George, Auntie Connie, Aunt Frances, Aunt Helen, and your cousins, too."

And then my dad: "Mike, I brought your favorite Mets cap with me." I later learned he hung it on the bed frame near my head.

Then I heard a new voice. It was confident and soothing. This was the neurologist who saved my life, Dr. Mulford. He was speaking to my family—the Krysiuk team. I couldn't make out his words, but I would eventually find out that Dr. Mulford thought very highly of my dad, mother, and sister, the way they stuck by my side, never giving up, always looking for new ways to help bring me back. My father learned everything he could from Dr. Mulford, reading medical journals, and keeping a watchful eye on the treatment I was receiving. He also did his best to make sure no nurse slipped up in keeping watch over me. One small mistake could cost me my life. Dr. Mulford believed my family's faith, optimism, and persistence were the most important factors in my recovery. At the time, I didn't hear the details of my physical and mental status. If I did, I don't know how it would have affected me.

But this is what I was told later that Dr. Mulford said, "I have good news and bad news."

My mother stepped up to the plate: "Bad news first, please."

"The bad news is that Mike sustained severe brain stem damage, and if he survives, he will be a quadriplegic for the rest of his life."

There was a shocked silence as my family stared down at me—motionless in the bed.

My sister cleared her throat: "What could possibly be the good news?"

"With any injury like this, there is always that chance, no matter how slim, of Mike recovering some body functions. But with brain stem injuries, you never know what areas will come back, if any at all. So, I am not going to promise you anything. It is definitely a crapshoot. But there is always that person who defies the odds."

My dad interjected now, "Is it good that Mike was physically fit and an athlete before he got in the accident?" The doctor just nodded. My father went on: "Mike isn't a quitter. He always perseveres to accomplish anything he sets his mind to."

"Yes," Dr. Mulford answered, "Sounds like he had a solid foundation to build on. But only time will tell…."

"How much time?" My mother pressed for an answer, "How long must we wait for Mike to come out of this coma?"

"It's impossible to predict. It could be five hours, five days, five weeks, five months…." My mother gasped. "We don't know." Dr. Mulford shrugged, looking almost apologetic. "Just spend time with your son. Talk to him every day. He's in there—let him know you're here, too."

Once again, my family looked down at me, probably wondering if I'd heard any of this conversation. But I hadn't.

I felt my mother's cool hand touch my face. "Where is our boy, Dr. Mulford? Where is he?"

"At a crossroads…."

"Crossroads?" She repeated back.

"That place between life and death."

Their voices faded to a hum. And that hum turned to TV static as my mind started changing channels again.

I wish they could all see what was unfolding in my head! I found myself running on a big field of green grass. Boy, was it long and brightly lit, not a cloud in the sky! I was running barefoot, but as if on air, because the grass was so soft it felt like I was treading on clouds. I was happy I didn't hit any rocks or glass. I didn't see the sun in front of me, so it had to be behind me, which meant there should have been my long dark shadow on the ground, moving in front. But I didn't see it. I had no shadow! This was confusing, but I kept running anyway. I wasn't even breathing hard. I felt completely refreshed. I wondered, with all these things going on, from the shifting channels to the long green field, and the feeling of dancing across the clouds, if I was actually running to heaven. *But it can't be? I have school in the morning, and I worked so hard for this—I have to hand that paper in! And all the friends I made! I'm becoming a popular guy. And not to mention those potential girlfriends waiting in the wings! C'mon, please God, I feel I'm on the right path now, I handed in all my work. And what about Susan? I was going to ask her out! Give me the chance! Give me the chance! I remember her brother wanted to kill me at Mario's the other day....*

All of a sudden the channel shifted, and I was revisiting the past. The green field morphed into a street that ran opposite the train station, and I was running towards Mario's. I burst through the front door and stopped in my tracks. I was looking at myself doing the end of night clean-ups with Ted and Dave. I had no memory of being in an accident. It was like I was watching reruns on TV. We were each doing our own little job. Ted was folding the napkins. Dave was filling the salt and pepper shakers. And I was taking the dirty dishes into the kitchen. I followed myself through the swinging doors.

It was bright, hot, and noisy back there. The bartender walked in, and I heard him say to Susan, "Can I have one more salad for the bar?"

She looked up from the salad station: "Okay, last one."

I put my bin in the dishwashing area and then paused to watch Susan toss the greens. The bartender watched her, too. The difference was, I couldn't keep my eyes off her. It was almost as if those leaves were falling in slow motion; no one could toss a salad like Susan! She was the one girl I wished was mine. But, as you know, every time I tried to speak to her, my tongue felt like it was swelling up, and I couldn't get a word out. I guess it was a lack of confidence…but I definitely had potential!

I did spit a few words out: "That salad looks…" but as I smiled at her, hunting for the words, Fred, the head chef (and also her older brother) approached me with a raised wooden spoon as if he were about to hit me over the head. The only word I could find to finish the sentence was "…green." That made Susan laugh.

Ted and Dave walked in.

The bartender turned to us: "I got tips for you three musketeers."

He pulled cash out of his pocket and counted it into our hands. Ted and Dave pocketed theirs right away. I re-counted mine carefully.

Ted had no patience for that, "Quit counting—you ready to go, moneybags?"

I checked it one more time. I was always proud and conscientious of my earnings.

"C'mon, La Craze!" Dave was getting pissed.

The backdoor stood propped open to ventilate the kitchen. I followed Ted and Dave out into the alleyway. My ghostly self stood only a few feet away, watching the scene unfold.

Ted punched me in the shoulder, "Why don't you go back in there and ask her out?"

"What, are you crazy? I value my life," I stared at him.

"What are you scared of? What's the problem?" He leaned against the brick wall, arms crossed, and just glared at me.

"Fred might pick up a knife next time instead of a spoon."

"Oh, c'mon, La Craze." Now Dave punched me in the arm for emphasis. "We got your back."

My arms were getting sore, so I said, "What the hell—what do I have to lose?"

I went and stood in the open doorway. I could see Susan cooling off in front of the kitchen fan. It made the back of her ponytail dance in the breeze. I looked over my shoulder at my friends, "Are you with me?"

"Yes," Dave said, "right behind you."

And Ted smiled.

Just then, Susan turned: "What's up, Mike?"

"Um," I searched for the words, "I'll see you tomorrow at school. Maybe meet you in the cafeteria for a soda...?"

Before she could answer, Fred shouted from across the kitchen: "What the hell are you doing there? Don't bother my sister. She has a lot of clean up to do before she goes home."

I was tongue-tied. Then Ted whispered in my ear: "Tell him this—"C'mon, I ain't talking to you, so cool it, man.""

I repeated this phrase, empowered by his attitude: "C'mon, I ain't talking to you, so cool it, man!" My voice didn't sound as confident as Ted's.

Fred took a few menacing steps toward me.

Ted fed me a few more lines. I repeated after him: "Oh yeah, look at that big tough guy--what are you going to do against us three?"

I wished I could warn myself to stop talking. *Bad idea*, I thought as I watched my pre-accident self standing there whole and healthy. *Big, big mistake!*

And just as I predicted, Fred grabbed a huge knife out of the butcher block, but at the last second stabbed it straight down into the cutting board. It stood there—quivering. That was Ted and Dave's cue to exit. I heard their feet pounding as they hightailed it out of there, leaving me standing all alone, facing Fred's wrath. I couldn't believe they'd left me! Fred was a high school linebacker. He rushed me like he was about to make the game-saving tackle.

I heard Susan yell, "Run!"

And I did.

I burst down the alley. All I could hear was my sneakers hitting the pavement, and Fred shouting, "Where the hell you think you're going? Come back here, you big chicken!" His voice echoed off the brick walls.

But I kept running through the parking lot, finally sliding under a car. I lay on my stomach on the cold asphalt and held my breath, trying not to make a noise. I could see Fred's boots approaching. He stopped a few feet from my hiding spot and shouted into the night: "I'll let you go this time, Krysiuk—but I'll see you at work tomorrow, you little…" he grumbled something at the end that didn't sound very good.

I could hear my thoughts again. I kept saying: *Holy Shit! Why me? Why now?*

Finally, Fred left. I waited until there was total silence, and then I crawled back out. I saw my former self look frantically around the parking lot. My troops had deserted me. Cowards!

I called out in a loud whisper: "Ted? Dave? Where's my team?"

No answer. Just the night breeze, and a few stars out. So much for a ride home, and it was getting chilly. I walked the mile back to Oak Ridge Park. My mother had left the porch light on, illuminating my path to the door. Only I wasn't able to follow myself in and see my family again; the channels were changing too fast.

I was back on that green field, running and running towards my destiny—a blue horizon—but there was still no sun overhead or shadow moving on the ground before me. It was all so confusing, but I just kept going. I felt I didn't have enough time to figure it all out. I was running for my life.

CHAPTER THIRTEEN

The next morning, my father came alone to the hospital. My mom and sister stayed home, contacting relatives and friends, filling everyone in. They were planning on seeing me later in the day. As my father walked down the hall toward the ICU, he ran into Ted's father, George. He was a tall, clean-cut man, part of the upper echelon of Westport—country club all the way. My dad stopped. Their eyes locked.

George cleared his throat nervously: "How…how's Mike?"

"He's in the ICU…in a coma. The doctors are trying everything to bring him back. I'm heading there now. And Ted?"

For a moment George looked down, then back up, a look of deep concern and pain in his eyes. "I am so sorry to hear the shape he's in." He paused, wrestling with the guilt of what he was about to say next. "Ted's stable. They are keeping him here, running some tests. He's got a few bumps and bruises, had some stitches…but it looks like he might be released soon. Please keep me updated on Mike's condition, and let me know if there's anything we can do."

My father nodded, and they parted ways.

When he came to my room, he sat down in the chair facing my bed and said, "Good morning, Mike. How are you today? Everybody says hello." Then he took the paper out and started reading, "The Yankees won last night—eight nothing. They played a good game."

Then I started drifting again. I saw that damn blue sky once more…and then I heard female voices. They were talking about some numbers, like they were monitoring something.

I heard, "MIke's levels are good today."

Mike? Mike who? They must have been talking about me! They must be the nurses…their voices are so beautiful…angelic.

The next thing I heard was, "How was your date last night?"

The other voice cut in, "That lazy son of a bitch—I'll never see him again unless to kick him in the ass."

"Oh, so I guess you didn't have a good time?"

Laughter filled the room, then I started drifting again. More blue sky, endless green field…then I heard my sister's voice:

"Hey, bro, how are you today?"

I guess everyone keeps asking me that question. I can't wait to answer them sometime…. At this point, I heard her call for a nurse: "Nurse! Nurse—he's having a convulsion!"

I came to learn later that my body would have a complete muscle spasm. It would tighten from head to toe, like the worst cramp you ever had in your life, everything stretched taut like a rubber band, pulled so tight it felt like I was about to snap. But being in a coma, I not only made no sound, I also had no control over my body's reactions.

A nurse said, "There's nothing we can do. It's just what the body does in a situation like this. You can't tell when it will happen or control it. We just try to make it as comfortable as possible for your brother."

As all this was happening, the days were moving along, like sand drifting through an hourglass, grain by grain. I heard my father's chair scraping as he pulled it up to the bed.

Then his voice: "Hi Mike. Today is April 8th, 1974. You've been in a coma for ten days." Then I heard the paper rustle, and he said: "Get a load of this—Henry Aaron ended the great chase tonight and passed Babe Ruth as the leading home run hitter in baseball history as he hit number 715 before a national television audience and 53,775 persons in Atlanta Stadium. The forty-year-old outfielder for the Atlanta Braves broke the record on his second time at bat, but on his first swing of a clamorous evening." There was a pause as if he was waiting for my response.

Then I heard a female voice, "We're going to check on Mike now."

I had no idea what they were doing.

Finally, my father continued: "It was a soaring drive in the fourth inning off Al Downing of the Los Angeles Dodgers, and it cleared the fence in left-center field, 385 feet from home plate. Can you imagine sitting in the stands when he did that...? Skyrockets arched over the jammed stadium in the rain as the man from Mobile trotted around the bases for the 715th time in a career that began a quarter of a century ago with the Indianapolis Clowns of the old Negro leagues." He sighed, then folded the paper. Now he shifted to a new subject: "Mike--your aunts and uncles and cousins are all stopping by, asking about you. And your Aunt Kash called from Florida. She says you know how you love fresh oranges? She's going to send you a whole crate full of them when you come...home."

I believe I spasmed after that. I learned later my father always rubbed my legs during one of these events.

Now a new voice was in the room, and I recognized it immediately—Ted. "Hello, Mr. Krysiuk." He sounded tentative. "How's Mike?"

"He's still here. He's fighting to come back to us, Ted."

There was a heavy silence, then, "I am so sorry, Mr. Krysiuk."

"Just say a prayer for Mike that he comes back to us quickly."

"Ok, Mr. Krysiuk.… Would it be all right if I talked to him alone?"

'Sure, I'll step out for a moment."

I heard footsteps retreating.

Then Ted's voice again, closer: "Hey, Big One…the gang says hello. And we're hoping you'll come back to us real soon.…" A long, pregnant pause. I think I heard him gulp nervously. Then his voice returned, more animated: "Remember those basketball games over at my house? We were shooting for beers. Those were great games! But we almost never finished 'cause we got so mad at each other. I wish you would wake up and tell me that everything is going to be alright. I wish.…" Ted started crying. It was hard to hear what he said next, but it sounded like, "Oh, dear God…" Then he took a ragged breath. "Please…bring him back NOW. I'll do anything. Please, please…ANYTHING!" At that moment my dad must have walked back into the room because I heard Ted say, "Mr. Krysiuk, he's so skinny. What's happening to him? And why is his fist stuck against his shoulder?"

"Take a deep breath, Ted. Relax. Mike's going through hell right now. He's lost a ton of weight, down from 180 to sixty-six pounds. And his spine stretched—that happens when you're stuck in bed. The doctors said he's two inches taller now—6'6". And since he's right-handed, one of the spasms broke that slat on his arm. The doctors decided to leave his fist up there by his shoulder for now."

"Oh, Mr. Krysiuk, I'm so sorry…I wish it was me instead of Mike."

A pause. All I could hear was the beeping of monitors. Then my dad's reassuring voice.

"It's OK, Ted. Just remember Mike the way he was and pray for his recovery."

"I will.… I promise."

A silence, and then, "Goodbye Mr. Krysiuk."

"Goodbye, Ted."

I heard Ted walk to the door, then pause, I imagine looking back at me. "Goodbye, Buddy."

CHAPTER FOURTEEN

Lying in a bed, not moving for seven weeks, turned me into quite a sight. I looked like a skeleton wrapped in skin. I was so thin I lost everything except my life. No part of me could move, except in a spasm. The nurses had to buzz my hair to keep the area clean around the burr holes as they healed. I was pale as a newborn. And those spasms arrived on their own schedule.

But no matter how bad it looked, or what was going on, my father stayed optimistic and came to see me every day. He took an indefinite leave from work, despite the financial stress it caused, to focus just on me. He read from the paper every day and always said encouraging words like, "Can't wait for you to come back...everyone says hello.... your ball-playing friends are holding a spot for you on the team."

My sister also came every day, and my mother when she could (it was hard for her). They would share the family news or things happening at school. Sometimes they updated me on current events. I don't recall the details of what they spoke about except this one time Maryann seemed to be reminiscing.

I heard her say, "I keep thinking back to when I was nine and used to organize the milk cartons in the church cafeteria before school started—eleven white and ten chocolate per tray—and then I'd walk with the nuns up the hill to the classroom. I was so proud to carry their books. There was this one time I shouldered my favorite nun's bag, and we were talking. I stopped halfway up. It was snowing and so cold.

I turned to her and said, 'I am going to have a baby brother one day.'

'Well, how do you know this?' She stared at me funny, with all that snow blowing in between us.

'Mommy says she can't have children anymore, but I just know things…I get these feelings.'

'Feelings…? Well, that would be a miracle now, wouldn't it?'

And I was right. One year later, you were born—January 15, 1957—my miracle brother! And you're going to be a miracle again, Big One. I feel it…"

Then her voice faded out, and I found myself back on that long stretch of grass, running and running toward a horizon it seemed I would never reach. I became very frustrated and agitated from those spasms and searching for that damn sun—which I hoped I'd see some time.

Then something happened—I can't say exactly when—but while running on that grass, I heard a soothing voice speak to me. It wasn't loud, but I could hear every word, very distinctly.

The voice said: "Michael, stop your running." I froze. "Go back…." I stood there now, listening. "No longer walk in peoples' shadows. Walk in your own light. Don't be a follower anymore. You have to shoot for the sun in everything you do, because even if you miss, you will land among the stars…and that is a GREAT place to be."

At that moment, I looked at the horizon, and the sun rose slowly into the sky—a perfect, yellow beacon. I felt like it was speaking to me: *Slow down, Michael. Enjoy the ride called your life. Don't run through it....*

And then I felt my eyes open.

I saw this strange ceiling above me. There were metal structures and tubes dangling. I couldn't move a muscle, but my eyes darted back and forth, searching for something familiar to focus on. But I could not find a single thing. And the reason I couldn't move a muscle was because I had become a quadriplegic.

All of a sudden I heard a voice. "Look! His eyes are open!" It sounded like my sister.

"Yes! Mike's back!" That was my dad talking. "I knew he'd make it!"

There was a commotion in the room. I think I heard my mother's rosary fall—beads rattling across the floor. I wanted to run through every door and shout through every window this amazing news—"The Big One is back!" But to spread this message, I knew I had my work cut out for me. This moment marked the official beginning of my recovery.

And it was to be a long road filled with hills, valleys, and many potholes. Large ones. Like when my sister came to visit me one day. She happened to be there at the time I was being fed. She could tell the young nurse was not very confident, so she watched her with an eagle eye. As the nurse attempted to maneuver the tube so I could eat, I started choking. The nurse froze, too new at her job to know what to do. I wished I could call for help, but I couldn't because I had a trach.

Maryann ran out to the nurse's station, shouting: "My brother's CHOKING! He's turning BLUE! Get somebody in here who knows what they're doing, NOW!"

The head nurse jumped to action, running with Maryann back into my room. Thank God she knew what to do to fix the tube and clear it out. My skin slowly returned to its normal color.

Meanwhile, my sister got on the phone. "Dad--you better get up here right away. Mike was choking. He turned blue. Some new nurse feeding him didn't have a clue what she was doing. And his breathing tube clogged. If I wasn't here, I don't know what would have happened. I got the head nurse and straightened everything out. But I think you better get up here and talk to these people--set them straight."

When my dad arrived, I'd been moved from intensive care to special care. My father immediately spoke with the head nurse.

I heard him say in a stern voice, "We've come so far with Mike--we DON'T want to go backward. Please have nurses in here that know what they're doing. It's OK to have nurses learn, but I don't want my son to be the patient they're learning on. Are we straight?"

"Yes, Mr. Krysiuk. I will take care of this personally. Mike will never eat alone again. He will have two of our best nurses at his side during the entire feeding."

As days passed, things started to go back to normal for me. My trach was removed, and my sister styled my hair, which was growing back in. Also, I slowly got movement back in my body through those muscle spasms. Though they were very painful, they were a signal I had life back in my body again. My weight was slowly returning as well since I now ate solid food and a steady regime of my mother's vitamins and nutritional shakes.

My dad would come in every day and talk to the therapists and learn what he could do to help. My father massaged my legs and arms. Slowly, I got some movement back in my limbs. As time went on, my dad made sure to come in every day. He knew I was very ticklish on the soles of my feet, so he would enter my room and pop his thumb against my heel, until one day, to his great excitement, my leg spasmed. This marked the start of getting movement back in the rest of my body. And this is when the therapist and my father started to go to work on me.

CHAPTER FIFTEEN

Therapy to me was like being a newborn babe, having to learn everything from scratch. My slate was wiped clean. I had to re-draw my picture. It began with a regime of exercises done while lying in bed. First, I had to lift my arms. The therapist taught me to connect a verbal command to a physical action.

She would say, "Raise your right arm and touch your nose with your index finger." And sometimes I would accidentally touch my ear. That made me very frustrated. I lost all my muscles and coordination. I had to re-teach my body how to move and where to move to. Nothing was effortless. I had to think out each move before I attempted to do it. I would have to picture it in my mind before I even moved an inch.

The blow to my head erased all my memory of how to coordinate my body. I would sit propped up in my bed and watch the way people walked or moved their arms. I would closely observe the way nurses picked up a glass or handed me something. I would memorize this motion and then attempt to copy it. I tried to make these actions appear natural and fluid, as they were in the past. Something as basic as scratching my nose or folding my hands together had to be studied and worked at endlessly.

My father would stand at the side of my bed and say, "Watch and copy me." Then he would touch his cheek and say out loud, "I am touching my right cheek," or "I am touching my left cheek."

He took the time to do this with every single part of the body. I would try to engrave in my memory the motions of my father, from touching his knees, elbows, hands, shoulders, legs, feet, and on and on it went. I had no sense of time. This re-training seemed to go on forever. If I touched the wrong part, he would simply say, in a kind voice, "Nope, try it again," until I got it right.

I wasn't able to speak in full sentences, more like two to three-word statements. I heard the whole sentence in my head, but I had to teach my mouth how to form the words. I studied the way people moved their lips when they spoke. My dad came up with an idea. He wanted me to read out loud. So he brought copies of Sports Illustrated to the hospital and would patiently sit there listening to me as I tried to pronounce each word. He knew I heard it in my mind and wouldn't rush me. It took patience and determination on my part, and my dad, mom, and sister wouldn't let me quit. They never even let the thought enter my mind.

I had to get every part of my body back, and the next step was standing up, even though one of my doctors had told my parents my chances of doing so were slim to none. Yet, from the exercises I'd been doing in bed, I'd already restored strength throughout my whole body. To regain the feeling of weight on my feet, the therapists brought in a stand-up table. I first had to roll out of bed onto a gurney. And the gurney was the stand-up table. There was a ledge to place my feet so they could rest flat on the ground, and a belt fastened around my waist so I wouldn't fall when they started to incline the table into a stand-up position. It reminded me of a laboratory in a Frankenstein movie, and I was the monster.

I don't remember how many times the exercise was done—but it was very painful, especially stretching my muscles and tendons. I not only screamed because of the pain but also from the fear of falling onto the hard floor with no coordination or ability to brace myself for impact. I dreaded the belt breaking. I was much taller than all the therapists. But they kept reassuring me it was safe. They gave me constant inspiration and confidence to believe in myself. To get through this ordeal, I would picture myself standing on the mound again, going through the windup, or planting my feet on the plate, ready to hit the ball out of the park. I wasn't about to give up. I was shooting for the sun.

The screaming only happened the first time. After that, I got through the pain and the fear with the help of my dad. He would talk to me the whole time they were moving me into the upward position: "It's going to take time, Mike, but it's like running a race—look at this as jumping over hurdles. You do it one hurdle at a time." Even when he wasn't there, I remembered what he said and kept repeating it in my head like a mantra. The more I exercised with the board, the stronger I became. And it always helped that my mom brought root beer popsicles, which were kind of like a reward.

The trainers had me wear special shoes with steel braces so my ankles wouldn't break. They were strapped all the way up my calves, and they had steel arches and heels. These boots acted as a crutch, helping me to regain my confidence and strengthen my legs. They were very expensive, and all my co-workers from Mario's, along with the owner, had thrown a fundraiser to buy them for me. I was just glad they couldn't see the hell I was going through when I first wore them. The whole process on the board with the boots took an hour—once in the morning and again in the afternoon. It was more exhausting than a baseball practice and a lot less fun.

Meanwhile, Ted had returned to school and resumed the motions of his life, going to breakfast with the gang, catching up on missed work (his father was coming down harder on him now), and sometimes listening to music and throwing back a few beers with the guys in his room. But he made the effort to visit during the times I was not in therapy, just relaxing in my room. He did this more than any other of my friends.

He tried to keep it light, sharing news about the Wreckers, girls, and school gossip. I'd listen quietly while squeezing the racquetballs my father had ingeniously placed inside women's stockings and tied to the frame of my bed. This exercise was slowly restoring mobility in my hands, which had been curled up in fists since the accident. The doctors were continually impressed with my dad's inventions.

One day, Ted said with a smile, "Susan's been asking about you."

My fingers froze, and I let the balls drop back into place.

"Hold it right there," I said. "I can't be thinking about girls right now. I got to focus on getting out of here."

We stared at each other a moment. I think he suddenly understood that we were now worlds apart. His blue eyes, once so mesmerizing, now seemed downcast.

"I feel bad about the way things turned out...." His voice was quieter than I'd ever heard it. "Should have been me—not you." Just then a nurse entered the room to check my vitals, providing a much-needed distraction. Ted stepped out of her way and stood against the wall. As she took my blood pressure, I watched Ted out of the corner of my eye. I could see that the accident had truly changed him. It was as if the guilt blanketed him now, giving him a heavy spirit. From what he told me, he was carrying on with his usual activities from school to girls, but something was missing. I could sense it, in both his voice and his actions. It seemed that terrible night was something he would never be able to outlive. And sadly, I was in no position to help him.

Meanwhile, my family was working on transferring me to a rehabilitation hospital. They had looked at the state hospitals and found them unacceptable. With no private rooms and patients that never seemed to leave, my parents knew I would never recover in such a place and have a chance at life. They wanted to find a rehab that could truly restore me and give me realistic hope. And that is how they found Gaylord, a private facility two hours away, but totally worth the travel and expense.

Before I moved to Gaylord, a few other friends came to see me and some of my cousins. They would make small talk and keep things light, but I could tell they were not comfortable seeing me in this state. They still remembered how I used to be…not how I had become. But I guess that's the price you pay when unexpected tragedy hits. I knew I was the same person inside, but I just could not react the way I used to. There was not only a motor delay, but I also couldn't even make jokes quickly. My mouth wouldn't form the words fast enough. And when I did get a joke out, I wasn't sure if they were laughing with me or just to humor me so I wouldn't get depressed or discouraged.

I told them, "This is just a pothole. When I come back from Gaylord, I am going to be pitching again on the mound. It's just a matter of time."

They would nod and say, "Don't rush yourself. You'll be back before you know it…." But I could tell they didn't believe what they were saying.

CHAPTER SIXTEEN

One day, Ted and his father came to visit after therapy. I was resting, watching the Yankees with my dad while squeezing my racquetballs; at this point my hands were really coming alive.

Ted pulled a chair up next to me, "Always exercising, huh?"

"You bet!" I answered, my eyes still glued to the game.

"I got a surprise guest for you. Guess who came up in the elevator with us?"

"What, Kaplan finally came to get his economics paper?"

"Kaplan, huh? I look like Kaplan? " Susan stepped through the doorway and everyone broke into laughter. She was like a fresh breeze blowing the tension out of the room.

"Susan! Oh, wow! Thanks for coming! Damn, I left my dance shoes at home—sorry we can't go party tonight."

She laughed, "Don't worry about it, Mike! I'll take a rain check." Susan stood at the foot of my bed, prettier than ever. I didn't even notice what she was wearing. All I could do was stare at her glowing face. The sunshine had arrived! And I thought to myself—*if only*…. "Everybody at Mario's says hello. They want to know when you're coming back."

"And your brother, too?" The memory of him chasing me was still fresh in my mind.

"He's out in the car. He drove me here and told me to tell you, if you ever need help when you get back home, he can get you some exercise equipment— whatever you need, Mike. He'll even come over and show you some workouts."

"Guess he's burying the kitchen knife. Tell him I'm forever in his debt. He's top-shelf on my list."

My dad chimed in, "Mike's going to Gaylord next week. That's when his road to recovery really begins."

"Yeah, I'm working hard. Going to play sports again...." I kept squeezing the balls furiously as I spoke.

Ted smiled, something I hadn't seen him do in a long time. "Shoot for the moon, Big One."

"Nah, I'm shooting for the sun."

Ted gave me a high five. It wasn't easy to let go of the ball and high five him back, but nothing is impossible when a pretty girl's in the room.

Just then my mom walked in carrying a box of root beer popsicles. "Here's a new batch, Mike. I checked with the nurses, and the last box is all gone."

"Yeah, people kept stealing them," I laughed.

My mom stopped in her tracks, spotting Susan. "Who's your lovely friend here?"

"She works with me at Mario's—makes the best salads."

Susan laughed again, "Yeah, speaking of that, I have to go to work now. Got to toss those salads!"

"Will I see you again?" I tried not to sound disappointed by such a short visit. "I'm gonna be transferring up to Gaylord in Wallingford. Do you think Fred might take you there?"

She hesitated, "We'll see, we'll see…You just get better, Big One." Then, summoning her courage, she crossed the few feet from the foot of my bed to my side and gently squeezed my hand. "I mean it. Get better soon."

I looked up into those baby blue eyes, which seemed to have tears gathering behind them. Then she turned abruptly and was about to disappear out the door.

I pushed myself up in bed and called after her: "Hey, I got a rain check for that dance, right?"

She turned in the doorway and smiled back radiantly, "Sure thing, Mike. Sure thing…."

I watched my dad and George nod approvingly at her. My mom seemed happy a girl had come to see me.

And then Susan was gone.

CHAPTER SEVENTEEN

The last week at Norwalk Hospital went by in a flash. I was finishing up my therapy. Friends and relatives were coming by to wish me a speedy recovery. My parents and Maryann packed all my stuff in a suitcase—even the crucifix. And I made sure to bring those exercise balls to tie them onto the new bed at Gaylord.

My uncle Joe came to help. He was friends with the driver of the ambulance that would transport me. I was able to scuff off the bed, and then my dad and the therapists helped me into the wheelchair. At this point I weighed around 130 pounds and looked like a stick figure, so it wasn't that hard to lift me. My dad pulled my Mets cap over my head and I was ready to rock and roll. Uncle Joe was waiting outside, talking to the driver. When the glass doors opened and I was wheeled out, Uncle Joe turned and said to my dad, "Is he ready to go?"

"All set!"

"Uncle Joe, you're not driving, are you?" I awkwardly stuttered the joke out.

He smiled at me, "No, no, I'm riding shotgun."

My mom and Maryann were standing by. They were going to follow behind in my father's white Valiant. I didn't even have time to take in the beautiful June day. I hadn't been outside in a long time, but I was more focussed on making this journey to Gaylord. The therapists helped lift me to a standing position and then lowered me onto a gurney. It felt good to stretch out. Then I was maneuvered into the back of the ambulance, and my dad climbed in next to me. It was a small ambulance, and the bed was too short for my now 6'6" frame, so I had to ride with my legs bent. It was a little uncomfortable, but I was willing to deal with the pain to get there.

I had no idea what Gaylord would be like. All I cared about was taking the next necessary step in my recovery; I couldn't wait to get to this place that offered real hope.

As the ambulance pulled out of the parking lot, my dad said, "How do your legs feel?"

"Not so great."

"I'll get the driver to pull over at a rest stop, and then you can stretch them out."

"I'm up for that!"

As I lay there, I could only see a glimpse out the back window of green trees, blue sky, and lots of sunshine. It was vaguely reminiscent of my coma, but I knew I was fully awake. And I felt pumped. A fire was building inside me to get to Gaylord and do whatever it took to get back to living again.

I started humming to myself that Beetles tune, "Get back, get back, get back to where you once belonged…" because that's where I was heading—my old life, my old self, strong and whole, the real me, The Big One.

Finally, we pulled over to a rest stop. The driver yanked open the back doors and with a sigh of relief, I stretched out my legs. A cool breeze ran over me, rustling my pant legs, which were bunched up over my shoe braces. It felt indescribably great, as if I was experiencing the wind for the very first time.

I turned to my dad, "Now I understand English class--*Paradise Lost*. Looks like I found it again."

He laughed. Then my mom and sister parked and walked over to us. My uncle got out of the ambulance and joined them.

When my mom saw my feet sticking out in those huge shoe braces, she said: "I guess they don't make ambulances for guys over six feet tall."

Maryann squeezed my leg, "We don't have much longer to go, Mike."

Then they all walked off a little ways and started talking. I overheard parts of their conversation.

Maryann was saying, "I have a good feeling about Gaylord. Mike's going to make progress there. They have a great track record, and I read up on all the therapy and rehab equipment."

Mom nodded, "This is the place for him."

And dad said, "The price is high, but we'll manage. We'll do whatever it takes, even if we have to sell the house. We just want to get Mike better."

And then it was time to close the doors and finish the last leg of my journey. I heard my dad say to Uncle Joe, "Did you see that look on Mike's face when he got that breath of fresh air?"

"Yeah, I saw it. Very encouraging."

The driver came round the side, "Sorry, Mike, got to hit the road again."

I scrunched my knees up, and he slammed the doors shut. A few minutes later, we turned back on the Merritt. I listened to the hum of traffic, and to keep my mind off the stiffness in my legs, recalled some of the pitches my father had taught me: knuckleball, curveball, change-up, sinker. As each one passed through my mind, my fingers twitched, trying to hold an invisible ball, to find the raised stitching, to feel the gritty leather, to grip my future, to believe....

CHAPTER EIGHTEEN

A half-hour later the ambulance took an exit off the parkway, and a few short turns later pulled up the long hill to Gaylord. *I'm on my way to recovery*, I thought. *I'm going to learn how to live my adjusted life.* Within fifteen minutes I found myself back in a wheelchair and pushed by my uncle through the rehab's shiny glass doors. I turned my head, looking left and right, wide-eyed like a tourist, eager to catch every new sight. "Looks like I've moved from the slums to fifth avenue!"

There were nurses in crisp uniforms bustling by and older patients sitting around in wheelchairs. I didn't see anyone my own age. There were one or two people who could maneuver with walkers and a few doctors striding by. I passed through more double doors, then down a long corridor. Everything in this area looked like how I'd imagined a college dormitory. Some of the doors were half-open, but I didn't focus on the patients resting inside their rooms—I just wanted to get to mine.

Finally, I was wheeled into a room in the middle of the hall. It was bright and clean and, most importantly, private. With some effort, I was shifted into the bed and sunk gratefully into my clean sheets. I could finally relax. *I made it*, I thought, as my head hit the pillow. My dad took my cap and hung it on my new bedpost.

"I feel like a ringmaster," I said to my dad, "let the rehab circus begin! I want to get out of here as soon as possible!"

A few minutes later, my mom and Maryann walked in.

My mom smiled with the first real joy I'd seen in a long time. "Everything is set."

Then Maryann added, "I picked out your menu. They have good food choices here—ten times better than Norwalk."

"Do they have root beer popsicles?"

"That's the first thing I asked. They even have those."

Everybody laughed. My mom walked over to the window. "This place is really worth the money. You get privacy Mike—and look at this view of the golf course. You wouldn't have this anywhere else—it's beautiful."

"I'll be playing golf someday—you can bet your money on it."

Just then a beautiful nurse walked in. She looked like Raquel Welch.

"Hi, my name's Donna. I'll be working this floor tonight. If you want anything, refreshments, or you need my help, don't hesitate to hit the call button." She pointed to the stand next to my bed. I looked at the red button and then up at my dad. He winked at me.

"Good thing I've been working with those exercise balls—my fingers are ready."

As if on cue, my dad pulled them out of the bag and tied them to the rails of the bed.

"Dinner's in thirty minutes." Donna smiled and left us alone.

Then there were hugs all around and my dad said, "You're in a good place now, Mike. We won't be back every day because it's a long drive. But we'll be here on the weekends." I liked the idea of independence. It made me confident that I was actually getting better.

So I smiled up at my dad and said: "I'm going to work hard, and when you come on the weekends, you'll see the positive improvements I made."

"OK, Mike." He had a big smile of approval on his face.

After they left, my first meal proved to be as good as Maryann predicted. It was a hamburger, French fries, and string beans. I quickly discovered that my therapy didn't start in the morning. It began immediately. As I stared down at my fork and knife, I realized that I was expected to feed myself—I was going solo. At Norwalk Hospital, devices were strapped to my hands with utensils secured in them. Now it was fully up to me to get the food into my mouth.

Slowly and carefully, I wrapped my fingers around the fork and tried to look as natural as I could as I speared a green bean. I didn't want to appear handicapped in any way. I was changing my middle name to "perfection." I was going to be smooth, graceful, normal. I lifted that first green bean to my mouth and didn't make one single mistake. This moment marked the first time I did a normal activity I once took for granted. Though that meal took a lot of concentration and determination to finish, when I was done, it felt like a victory.

When Donna came back and took my tray, she said, "Oh, I see you finished everything," and gave me a big smile as she walked out.

Now it was time to go to bed. I had filled my belly and could finally watch some TV before dozing off. I quickly learned that there were only three channels: the news, sports, and old reruns. *Green Acres, here I come!* But, then I thought, *I got a busy day tomorrow—I am going to cash in and get some rest.* So I turned off the TV and shut my eyes. Gaylord was much quieter than Norwalk. No loud voices or nurses coming in and out. It felt like a close version of being home. *Tomorrow, here I come!* And before I knew it, I was asleep.

CHAPTER NINETEEN

In the morning, Donna wheeled me into the dining area and said, "I am going to seat you with the Three Amigos—John, Mark, and Debbie."

My confidence was kind of shaky. I hadn't been around new people in a while. "Do you think they'll like me?" I asked.

"They are great people. Give them a chance. The one who looks like an overweight Don Knotts—that's John. He had a heart attack while he was playing golf. He's been here three weeks. And Debbie—the Dorothy Hamill look-alike—broke both legs in a car accident. She used to be a dance teacher. And Mark—he dresses and looks just like Walter Matthau from *The Odd Couple*. He shattered his right shoulder when he fell off a ladder cleaning the gutters for his wife. He never stops complaining about her."

"Wow, they're all a ton older than me."

"Don't worry about that, Mike—they're always happy to meet new people."

As Donna pushed me into my spot at the table, carefully avoiding John's quad cane, he looked at me over his glasses and said, "Welcome, kid! Roll right up and have the meal of a lifetime!"

Beside him, Debbie, mid-thirties, thin and athletic, sipped coffee with one hand, while resting the other on the top of her cane.

She smiled at me and said, "Yeah, we reserved this spot just for you. We're the Three Amigos."

Now Mark chimed in. He was wearing a Mets baseball jersey, number zero. He gargled his orange juice, then set it down.

"Yeah, we were looking for a fourth. C'mon, roll up. We don't bite. But watch out for Debbie here—we keep an eye on that one! Don't let her sweep you off your feet."

Debbie chuckled at this. "Oh guys, c'mon."

Donna moved on to do other things, and I was left with the Amigos.

I stared down at my knife and fork, then back at my new buddies and declared:

"I am going to *enjoy* this meal."

Then I picked up my fork, doing the best I could to look natural. I knew no one at this table or anyone in the room was judging me, which made it that much easier. I managed to cut a piece of my pancake and lift it slowly to my mouth. "Wow, these could make Aunt Jemima jealous!" They laughed. Inwardly I was thinking: *let the recovery begin!*

"You must have come from Norwalk Hospital—I hear their food tastes like cardboard." Debbie's eyes twinkled as she watched me eat.

"Right on target. So, Deb, where are you from?"

"I'm from Hartford. I'm sorry, but I won't be here that long to get to know you."

"What do you mean?"

"I'm going to be discharged tomorrow."

"How long you been here?"

"Three weeks. I came here in a wheelchair, and I will be walking out of here with a cane!"

John smiled at her teasingly: "And maybe do a little shuffle step— like on Broadway." Everyone laughed.

"Maybe a waltz. I'll start with the slow stuff."

Mark poured her some more coffee: "You go, girl!"

I slowly took a sip of orange juice: "Anything to warn me about before you go?"

"Except for these clowns—no. The therapists are great. They work with you, not against you. They are the best. They'll push you further than you could ever push yourself. And from that bright, positive look in those big blue eyes of yours, I know you're going to do well.

I blushed and managed to say, "Thanks…."

After breakfast, Marie, a middle-aged attendant, rolled me into the exercise room. It was a big space filled with therapists and patients. There were parallel bars, exercise mats, recumbent bikes, and different types of bars attached to the wall where patients were doing stretches and deep knee bends. Other patients were attempting to walk with quad canes, walkers, and single canes across the floor. Each person was accompanied by a therapist. There was a focussed atmosphere in the room, and occasionally I would hear therapists saying things like, "You can do this," or "Don't be scared. Have confidence in yourself." Though this place was far removed from the weight rooms and exercise gymnasium of my high school, I approached my new training ground with the same dedication and determination I used in varsity sports. The only thing that was missing was the coach's whistle. And of course, most of the patients in here had white hair except me. I was by far the youngest in the room. I felt like a rookie. But I was ready to go!

Marie pushed me into a waiting area. There was a wheelchair in front of me and one behind. I was too focussed on the work ahead to make small talk. And everybody else seemed the same. They all possessed a focussed attitude toward exercising. This was not a country club! We were all here for the same reason—to get strong, then leave this place as soon as possible. A pretty, young therapist approached me. She looked around twenty-two, with a cute bob that framed her bright brown eyes.

"Hi Mike," she held out her hand. I took it, and she said, "Oh, that's a nice firm handshake."

"I've been working on squeezing exercise balls that my dad attached to the bed."

"That's great! Let's get started. My name's Sandy, and I'm your therapist. We've got a lot of work to do. Are you ready?" I took one more look around the room, for a moment feeling a little intimidated. She must have noticed: "Just think of me as your best friend—right by your side, every step of the way." Her words soothed my fears.

"Like my guardian angel?"

She just smiled and turned to Marie: "I got it from here."

As Marie walked off, I said: "Don't forget to tip the driver!"

Both women laughed. And then Sandy pushed me over to an

exercise mat that was really a ten by ten raised platform two feet off the floor. I stared at it with trepidation. "So, am I going to get on this mat?"

"Yes. I'll be right here, Mike. Don't worry. Nothing's going to happen. You just push yourself up, and I'll help you stand and move you over to the mat."

I took a deep breath and centered all my strength in my arms. With great focus, I attempted to push myself up. It took many tries to overcome the fear of falling because, when I did lose my balance, I could never control where my body landed. With strength, you gain coordination, and I still lacked the muscle tone to perform this task. In great frustration, I fell back into my wheelchair for the third time. "Damn! This is pathetic. I used to bench 300."

"It's OK. Stay calm. I'll help you up." She came around my side and said, "Try one more time." As I lifted myself, she put an arm under me and helped direct me to the mat. It took quite a few baby steps in my metal shoe braces with Sandy directing me the whole way to make a safe landing on that mat. When I did, she let go and I felt great!

"Awesome!" she said, "That was your first exercise—chair to mat."

I sat there thinking how I took these small actions for granted growing up—just being able to sit up and sit down. I mean, when does a child master these skills? I didn't even recall. Children learn by observation. I could picture how to move—I could see it in mind's eye—but I had to re-teach my body how to execute everything. It was like the natural flow between the brain and the body was disconnected. For every single thing I wanted to do, from lifting a fork to walking again, I had to carefully visualize and then command my muscles to perform the action. I was both anxious and excited to progress as quickly as possible.

As a seventeen-year-old athlete, my youthful adrenaline was starting to flow again. I couldn't wait for the next task.

I looked up at Sandy, "OK, what's next?"

She smiled. "We will work on balance. First, you will lie on your stomach. And then you will push yourself up onto your hands and knees."

"When does dancing start?"

She laughed. "All right, Fred Astaire—take it easy!" Then she helped guide me onto my stomach. I pushed myself to my hands and knees, succeeding on the first try. "Very good, very good." I was now on all fours. I caught my breath for a moment, watching all the old patients' walkers passing by. Then Sandy said, "I am going to do some strength exercises with you. I am going to push on your body, and you resist it. This way, you will gain strength in your limbs." She began to apply pressure to the side of my body. I felt like a football lineman holding my position. "Pick one hand up." I managed to do as she requested without falling over. "Now, pick up your leg." I was able to do that, too, staying focussed as if I was performing gymnastics. I mean, if you think about it, gymnastics is part of football.

This routine of moving from the wheelchair to the mat and then onto my hands and knees to do resistance training became the pattern for the next few days until Sandy surprised me one morning by saying, "You are now able to move to the parallel bars. You are going to stand up and learn to walk again."

I couldn't believe my ears. I knew I was progressing quickly because I'd overheard my father talking with Sandy the night before, and she'd said, "Mike is really moving at a fast rate. He has that athletic fight back in him to win." But I had no idea that the next day I would be shifting to the parallel bars and working toward walking again. That was my dream—to walk…and more! As I was wheeled toward the parallel bars, I felt as if a ray of sunlight was falling on me.

CHAPTER TWENTY

I was now strong enough to push myself out of the chair and grab onto the parallel bars. Sandy had secured an exercise belt with handles on it around my waist. She used this to steady me as I reached for the equipment. The belt also increased my confidence. As my fingers wrapped around the rubber-coated bars, I felt a sense of elation. I moved my right boot forward. I tried to make this first step look as natural as possible. Then I moved the left. Step by step, I started to inch forward. I was staging a comeback. I was aiming for the goal. I was shooting for the sun. I felt like I was on my way home. It was just a matter of time.

What I learned later from my friends was that as I progressed, Ted was coming apart at the seams. I don't think he was ever able to process the accident and what happened to me. He just couldn't accept it. As the dark clouds lifted off of me, they seemed to settle on him. The responsibility and guilt of the accident were always on his mind. I heard from my father and sister that he was often seen riding his motorcycle around town with a dark look on his face, or hanging out with the gang at the diner but quieter than ever, or sitting by himself at some party. Perhaps he was always thinking about what happened to me and the price I was paying for the mistakes we made that night?

When he came to see me at Norwalk Hospital and also at Gaylord, he seemed unusually subdued; he really didn't communicate with me beyond small talk. He would sit there and nod and add little bits to the conversation, but he never really directed any question toward me. The days when we really talked were gone. It was like Ted couldn't relate to me in my current state. He was unsure how to react to my condition, the once smooth operator at a loss for words. He treated me like a piece of priceless crystal, not wanting to crack or shatter me by saying something wrong. He seemed to have a fear of throwing me into a depressed state of mind. But I was actually very positive. I was always shooting for the sun. Even though at this moment I could no longer play basketball or baseball, go out and have a beer with the boys, or raise a little hell, I remained completely focussed on picking up the pieces of my life to create a successful and functional future. Ted, on the other hand, seemed scared and stricken, tormented with the nightmare I would never recover. He took the blame straight to heart and just couldn't seem to shake it. No matter what he did, whether in school or work, alone or socializing, he seemed lost in the shadows.

But I was moving forward into the light. With my therapist at my side, I was building a physical and mental foundation that could support my recovery and re-entry into society. At Gaylord, the dream seemed possible as long as I kept my nose to the grindstone and did the work. I felt stronger every day. Within three weeks, I left the parallel bars and was able to walk across the room with a walker, and then I graduated to quad canes.

I had a limp like John Wayne, and I used to say to Sandy, "Where are the movie cameras and the agents now—I could be John Wayne's double!"

And she would laugh and follow alongside me as I moved fluently with my shoe braces and quad canes from one corner to the other, passing other patients and smiling at them as I went. Sometimes they smiled back, proud of my achievement.

One day I saw my dad watching me, all lit up with pride. I'd almost forgotten what he looked like when he was happy. He saluted me like I was a fellow soldier; it made me feel like all my hard work was finally paying off, and the dreams he held for me were becoming a reality. My sister came to stand beside him. She was beaming, too. But then I started wondering why they were there that day.   When I finished my session, we went to sit in the social room. Even though I could walk with quad canes, I was transported through the hospital in a wheelchair. My dad pushed me into the common area where patients were playing cards, reading books, doing crossword puzzles, and talking in low voices. We took a seat by the window.

My sister turned to me and said, "Before we came to see you in therapy, we had a meeting with your doctor and therapist. And there's good news. In three weeks, you will be discharged and start outpatient physical therapy in Stamford." I could not believe my ears!

"I'm leaving in three weeks? Wow!"

"Yes, and you'll be coming home for the next two weekends," my father jumped in, "And the third weekend, you will be coming home for good. Everyone is really impressed with your progress. You've reached the next stage."

"And you won't believe what dad's done for you," Maryann exclaimed. "He's spent weeks creating an exercise area in the basement for you. We got a rowing machine donated from the New Canaan YMCA.

It had a broken oar that Dad fixed, and now it's working beautifully. He's also been busy inventing stuff to rebuild your body—you'll see."

I looked at my dad. It was like I was really seeing him for the first time since the accident. Though I noticed that the stress had deepened some of the lines on his forehead, there now seemed to be a light in his hazel eyes. He looked refreshed, like the clouds were finally parting. He reached over and squeezed my shoulder.

"We'll be home soon."

Those last three weeks went by pretty fast, especially because I could now go on field trips with some of the other patients. One week we drove in a van to a nearby lake. The attendants would press a button on the side of the vehicle, and a lift would lower us in our wheelchairs to the ground. Then we were pushed to the edge of the water.

As my wheels hit the grass and I stared at that green, algae-filled lake, I felt a sense of living again. The breeze blew fresh off the water, but I couldn't smell anything due to the accident. The blow to my head removed my sense of smell but not my ability to taste food—thank God! I did take pleasure, however, in staring up at that blue sky and feeling the bright sun hit my skin. The heat revived me. To my left and right, the other patients seemed equally excited. I saw them looking around and growing almost giddy.

Once at the edge of the lake, a fishing pole was placed in my hand, all baited up and ready to go. Growing up, I always fished on the dock downriver from our house. We also had an eighteen-foot speed boat that my father and mother took me fishing on. My sister also came on occasion. Those were happy days. And now the good times were returning. Maybe I couldn't throw that rod as hard as I used to, but I managed to fling out that worm and watch it drop in the water. I didn't catch anything that day except a bunch of green stuff. Nobody did. I held up my rod and said, "Guess the 'sharks' are lucky!" My fishing companions laughed.

Next, we went bowling. The van transported four of us to the local alley. I sat in the wheelchair facing the pins. A small, wooden ramp was placed between my legs. I didn't care who was in that bowling alley watching me. As I pushed the ball down the ramp as hard as I could and watched it roll towards the pins, I felt a sense of real success. Sometimes the ball hit, sometimes it missed. But all I cared about was having fun outside the hospital and being back in society again. I don't remember what my score was, but I think the gutter won!

On the first weekend I was released to go home, I participated in a special tradition that Gaylord established for patients. There was a small stuffed monkey that was passed from one rehabilitated person to the next when they left. It had been handed to me by a twenty-five-year-old woman recovering from a severely broken leg. Two weeks into my stay at Gaylord, the attendant seated her at my dining table. She immediately reached across and set the monkey down in front of my plate. I stared at the small stuffed animal with the beady eyes, then back at her.

"What's this?" I said.

"*This* is the Gaylord hand-me-down monkey. It brings good luck. It was given to me when I first got here. And now I'm giving it to you. When it's your turn to go home, you keep it in circulation, OK? Find someone you want to encourage."

"Will do. I promise!"

And now it was *my* turn to pass the monkey on. The day before I left, I decided to give it to a boy who also played high school sports. He'd broken both legs in a bad car accident. Watching him wheeled around the facility with an anxious, frustrated look on his face, I could relate, so I went by his room and knocked on the door. "Come in," he said, sounding a bit depressed. I rolled in, the monkey balanced on my lap, and stopped at the side of his bed. He turned to me, a funny half-smile lighting up his face.

"Hey Mike, whatcha got there?"

"I have *the* famous Gaylord good luck monkey. I'm passing it on to *you* because I will be leaving for my first weekend home tomorrow." I held it up in the air like a trophy. "This little guy's got the power. I'm now bestowing that power upon you." When I said those last words, I stared him dead in the eye. We both must have looked pretty serious, but then we both broke into laughter. Spontaneously, we reached up and gave each other a high five. I placed the monkey ceremoniously on his bed and said, "Hope you will be giving this magic monkey to someone else soon." And then I rolled out.

The next morning, my father and sister came to pick me up. As the attendant pushed me through the sliding glass doors into a bright summer day, I felt a sense of freedom I hadn't known in a very long time. There was not a single cloud in the sky. The sun beat down on me, and I could feel the heat through my Mets cap. I stood up out of my wheelchair and was able to maneuver into the front passenger seat. Maryann drove. My dad was in the back. As we headed down the hill from Gaylord and turned onto the Merritt, I was like a kid in a candy store looking all over the place. I was out! I was back in action! I was going home!

CHAPTER TWENTY-ONE

As we turned down Oak Ridge Park, I noticed bright balloons tied to a telephone pole near my house. As we pulled into the driveway, I could read the handmade signs: "Welcome Home Big One," "You're number 1," and "Keep shooting for the sun!" The last time I saw the maple tree in the front yard, it was turning that bright spring green. Now the leaves were faded by summer heat, and the trunk festooned with ribbons. My mom's flower beds were thick with tulips and hydrangeas, everything in full bloom, carefully tended by her green thumb. Home looked totally perfect—better than I ever remembered it. I was noticing things I never realized were there before, like how expertly manicured the grass looked, now mowed by my father in razor straight lines, and the beautiful stone flower pot he designed for my mother on the front porch, filled with her famous heirloom roses. And something new—my father had constructed a wooden ramp leading up the stairs to the front door so I could be wheeled right in.

My father opened the car door, and I swung my feet out. My teenage cousins, Rich and John, were standing there, staring down at my huge metal braces. Behind them, I saw my Uncle Joe in his Yankees cap looking on. Beside him stood my cousin Patty, a free-spirited twelve-year-old with a huge smile. Her older sister, Nancy, was there, too. We were the same age, and she was also an athlete—co-captain of the high school field hockey team. My Uncle John stared at me with excitement. He was still in his carpentry overalls that were now stained from gardening (he boasted the biggest and best vegetable garden in town), and my Aunt Frances smiled at his side—a pretty blonde with a big heart who always gave us kids popsicles on a hot day when I was growing up. They all looked so happy on the surface, the way the ocean can sparkle on a summer day, but underneath, I sensed the deep undertow of pain and concern as they took in my present condition.

To put them at ease, I said, "Only temporary, only temporary—let the party begin!"

At this, they all smiled, and Rich shouted: "The Big One's back!"

My Uncle Joe snapped back to life and ran to pop the trunk. He pulled out my wheelchair, and as he unfolded it, everyone grew quiet again.

"Like I said, this is just temporary—my new set of wheels."

Rich snickered, "So, where's your license?"

And John chimed in, "License—he doesn't even have a learner's permit yet!"

"Yeah, I won't need a license—I won't have it that long!"

Now the tension was really gone; everyone laughed, and as I plopped down into the wheelchair, a big family cheer broke out and my cousin Nancy shouted: "Welcome home, Mike!"

My dad wheeled me up the ramp and through the front door, which was propped open.

As I entered my living room, I looked up at my dad and said, "This has been a long time coming. I've dreamt of this moment, it seems like forever…and now it's finally come true." Then I stared at all the family members and friends who had gathered there for me. To the crowd of radiant faces, I declared: "I'm going to work hard to stay home and start to live my life again."

My dad's voice was firm and positive: "You're more than halfway there, Mike. It's just a matter of time."

I stared at the dining room table; it was spread with a huge feast. My mom had gone all out—everything from salads to sandwiches, chips, popcorn, dip, and even a plate of big chocolate chip cookies—my favorite. Hospital food was edible, but this was gourmet!

Patty leaned down, "What can I get you, Mike?"

"The house special—your choice."

She headed for the table and grabbed me the first plate. I watched her pile it up with a little bit of everything. My dad pushed me over to the table, and before taking that first bite, I looked around and soaked in the moment. Everyone was in a great mood, talking, laughing, and it felt good to be back. *All I have to do now is get back in shape physically, so I can recover from this damn accident. Shit! Why me? Why now…? If this is a nightmare, let me wake up…. No, this is for real. And I have my work cut out for me. Like my dad said, it will just be a matter of time …. I have to keep shooting for that sun.*

At that moment the doorbell rang. Maryann went to get it. Ted and Jim walked in, followed by Dave, Brian, and Barrett.

I heard Maryann say, "Hello, boys! Come on in. The Big One's back! He'll be thrilled to see you."

They greeted my parents then walked toward me. They all had big smiles, but I could sense they felt uncomfortable seeing me in a wheelchair. Ted led the way. He gave me a high five, then everyone copied him.

"Welcome home," he said.

Maryann came over, "If you're hungry, boys, grab a sandwich."

"Welcome to the party!" I held up a cookie, "You should try these, they're great!" People got up, making room for my friends. Ted stood back a little from our gang, watching them grab food. I looked up at him, "C'mon Teddy boy—step it up! Have your fill!" He didn't respond. "C'mon, don't be shy, it won't bite you." Finally, he loosened up and grabbed a plate.

I watched my friends. They ate in silence. I didn't really know what to say, so I sat quietly and enjoyed the moment. I wanted to get out of that wheelchair and sit in a comfortable seat in the living room like I used to before this whole damn thing happened. So I turned to my buddies, "I am going to go sit in the living room in my favorite spot."

Ted paused, a cookie half-way to his mouth, "Want me to help you get over there?"

"Nope! I'm going solo on this one. I'm going to do the old butt shuffle."

I swiveled my chair, then lowered myself to the floor. It was fairly easy—my upper body was very strong from all the exercises at Gaylord. My friends just sat there watching. I could tell they were uncomfortable observing my acrobatics because they remembered me the way I was before the accident. The blow to my body had wiped my slate clean, forcing me to learn the simplest things I once took for granted. I'd done a pretty good job making all my motions look graceful as I ate those cookies, even with my limited coordination, but now I had to somehow find my way over to the easy chair by the fireplace, and I doubted that would look too smooth.

I was now on the floor facing the living room. I saw my mother and father look at me with some concern. My mom made a motion for my dad to come over, but instead, he put a hand on her arm, and I overheard him say, "No, this will make him stronger. Let him do it. He'll let us know if he needs help." The party seemed to come to a stop. Everyone was now staring at me. There were a lot of legs blocking my path.

"I'm heading for that chair over there. Make me a little opening—I'll shoot right through." People moved aside, and I started to scoot. My friends watched with the rest of the party. I could tell they had no idea what to say. If I were in their shoes, I probably wouldn't either. I must have been a sight doing the butt shuffle across the living room floor, but I didn't care. I had my sights set on that green easy chair. I kept my mind focussed on the comfort of those soft cushions to replace the hard wheelchair. It took me five awkward minutes to get there. I climbed up into that seat and plopped down as if nothing had happened. The moment my butt hit the cushion, I said, "Ta-da!" Followed by, "OK! Show's over!" I broke into a laugh with everyone else, and all the tension left the room.

"Way to go, La Craze!" shouted Dave. All my friends were happy, except Ted, who just sat there looking sad and uncomfortable. It seemed like he wasn't able to feel my positive energy at all. He brooded, probably blaming himself for turning me into a cripple, forced to crawl on the floor. I saw him push his plate away, his food mostly untouched.

I looked out the window at the maple, glowing in the fading light. People were starting to leave. I sat like a king in the easy chair, saying goodbye to each guest, thanking them for coming. A lot of the women were still helping my mother and sister clean up.

My dad brought my wheelchair over and said, "Hey, you guys want to go in the backyard while we finish up here? You can catch up for a little bit before you all head out."

"I'll push him," Jim offered.

"Watch out for the potholes," I laughed, maneuvering into the seat.

"Clear sailing all the way!" He pushed me fast to the front door.

"This is a wheelchair, not a boat!" I corrected.

Jim carefully got me down the ramp and wheeled me around the side of the house and across the grass. Jim was right—it was clear sailing. He parked me in the backyard under the floodlights. Barrett grabbed some folding chairs, and a circle was quickly formed around me. It was great breathing that fresh air (even though I couldn't smell the Saugatuck like I used to) and listening to the many sounds I once took for granted: the throb of cicadas, rustling leaves, even a dog barking somewhere down the street. I tried to think of something to say to my friends.

Finally, I piped up: "Hey guys, playing any basketball down at the beach this summer?"

Dave answered, "Nope, I'm bussing down at Crossroads—making good bucks. It already helped me pay for my motorcycle in cash. It's all mine now—running like a charm."

I smiled at him, "Hey, can I have a ride?" But my joke fell flat. Everyone sat gazing at me uncomfortably, and Ted looked the most agitated. He stared at me with those intense blue eyes, but I felt like he was actually looking inside himself, not truly seeing me. I tried to lighten things up, save the moment: "You mean you don't have a sidecar on that bike? C'mon Dave, I ain't gonna ride in a seat holding onto your butt!" It worked. They all broke out laughing. Even Ted gave a little smirk. Then Royce came around the side of the house, surprising us all.

"Hey, Royce! Pull up a seat." I motioned towards a chair. He grabbed it and plunked down next to me. I turned to him, "You still playing those drums? When I'm better, we'll jam again."

"You bet," his voice sounded reassuring, confident.

"I can't play any sports yet, but I bet I can still pick and grin—hey, can somebody go get my guitar?" Brian shot up right away. I called after him, "It's in my bedroom, my dad will show you where."

A few moments later, the best surprise of all happened. I heard some girlish laughter, and then Susan and Nicole came around the side of the house. I didn't notice the things about her I used to, like her polka dot sundress, pretty eyes, makeup, or long hair. I was just so happy that she came. That all of them had come. That I wasn't alone. Loneliness had been my closest companion in the hospital. It was the most hollow feeling I'd ever experienced in my life. Yes, I had my dad, my mom, and my sister…but it just felt like I needed more. I couldn't put the whole burden on my family to fill the void the accident had created. I needed the energy of people around me, especially those my own age.

Brian returned at that exact moment with my sticker-covered case. I don't know why I asked him to go get it. I knew deep down I couldn't physically or emotionally handle playing at this time. And now I had to try to make some music in front of Susan....

Ted ran to get chairs for the girls. "Hey," he said, positioning them opposite me, "Mike's going to serenade you." Susan looked expectantly at me. In the floodlights, her warm eyes seemed to shine even brighter.

"Oh, that's great." She put a reassuring hand on my arm.

Brian pulled out my instrument and handed it to me. I just sat there with the guitar laid across my lap. I didn't even bother tuning it. I just took a deep breath, then picked it up and strummed a few simple chords. It felt awkward. My mind remembered how to play much more complicated things, but my fingers were not cooperating. Royce watched me closely.

Then he said, "Don't worry Mike, you'll get it back over time. Don't push yourself."

That's when I put the guitar down. "Yeah," I tried to keep my voice upbeat, "when you hear me play next time, I'll be so good you'll have to buy tickets." Now I got a smile of support around my little circle.

As Susan helped me put my guitar back in the case, she said: "Make sure there's enough seats there because we're going to bring the whole gang."

Her words made me feel good—flattered to know that people had not forgotten me—the *real* me. This "in crowd" I had tried so hard to be part of was, ironically, accepting and taking notice of me at my lowest point. And all I had to do was just be myself. It seemed like Ted and the gang just wanted me to keep working toward getting back to the guy they'd known—mentally, physically, and socially.

I also used to be so worried about getting girls to look at me as the cool guy, but this damn accident had now put me center stage for all the wrong reasons. I knew Susan noticed me now, but it was more as an object of pity, not the crush I'd hoped for. If the relationship had once been heading toward a date, it was now thrown off the rails and mired in friendship. That was all I could hope for, I realized. But I gladly accepted her kind words and smile. And even Nicole helping Susan snap my case shut struck me as an act of friendship, which I sorely needed at this time. All those lonely months in the hospital had given me a new outlook on people. I knew that from now on, no matter who I met, I would greet them as a friend and not judge them on what they had or what they could do. Being a true friend was what mattered to me.

My mom came to stand under the lights. She looked a little tired but very happy. She addressed the crowd: "Thanks for coming by and welcoming Mike home. But we're going to have to call it a night. Mike's had a long day."

Ted stood up first: "Thank you, Mrs. Krysiuk." And the guys followed suit. Ten minutes later all the chairs were empty, and I was back inside, looking out the living room window as people drove off, beeping their horns goodbye.

Ted was the last to go. He'd wheeled me inside and now lingered for a moment at the front door. In his worn motorcycle jacket, blue eyes translucent in the porch light, he looked very much the brooding James Dean of a bygone era. He gave me a quick high five then grew somber. "I never told you this, but when you were first in the ICU Kaplan made a big announcement to the class. He said that you had died in the night."

"Wow...looks like Mr. Perfect got his facts wrong."

Ted didn't even laugh. His face looked flushed with anger, remembering. "I stood up and banged my fist on your empty desk and said, 'For once in your life you're wrong, Kaplan, The Big One's alive!'"

"Alive and kicking," I stuck out my boot and shook it.

Finally, Ted smiled. "I promise to help get you back on your feet, Mike. I'll come by tomorrow and you can show me all the exercise equipment your dad set up. And I won't let you slack off. If you do, I'll kick you in the ass."

"Deal." I watched him turn and run across the front yard and climb into the car with all my friends. Susan leaned out the window and yelled, "Bye, Big One!"

I called across the yard, "I'm gonna be discharged in two weeks. Maybe you could stop by...?"

My father came around the side of the house, carrying some chairs. I could see his face fall when she said, "I've been working a lot. Can't make any promises, but I'll be thinking of you, Mike."

As the car pulled away and sped down the street, I realized it was time to stop concentrating on girls and put all my focus on getting strong—body, mind, and soul. In my heart, I wished Susan well. But as the tail lights disappeared around the corner, I knew with sudden clarity she'd never be mine. I turned and wheeled myself back inside. For a moment, I watched my mother and Maryann balling up the tablecloth then polishing the wood underneath. My dad straightened the furniture and got the vacuum. Everything was as it should be—the rituals of home. And in two weeks I'd be back here where I belonged. A day would come when I could chase girls; I was sure of it. But for now the spotlight had to be on my recovery. The star—The Big One—was going to shine again!

CHAPTER TWENTY-TWO

When I woke up the next morning, I had slept so well I almost forgot my limitations and wanted to jump out of bed and grab breakfast. Instead, I lay there enjoying the morning sun peeping through my curtains. The house was still quiet and somewhere I heard my neighbor trying to start his old Buick.

At that moment, the door cracked open, and I heard my dad say, "Good morning, Mike. How are you feeling? You're up early."

"Pretty good." I sat up on my elbows and smiled at him. "Guess I'm still on the hospital schedule. I was just thinking about my buddies— all the good times we used to have. Ted and the guys are coming over later."

He approached my bed slowly. That's when I noticed he had a very sad, disturbed look on his face. For a moment he just stared at me, and I felt something was terribly wrong. When he spoke, his voice was flat.

"I have some bad news to tell you about Ted."

I froze. "What happened, Dad? Is he OK?"

"Last night there was a fire at his house." He paused, cleared his throat. "I'm afraid Ted didn't make it."

I lost my ability to speak. The room seemed to just fill up with silence. Then, like a gunshot, the neighbor's engine turned over—bang—and I heard him backing out. His car faded down the street, and then the neighborhood was quiet again—only the sound of morning birds.

Finally, I choked some words out: "No! It can't be! Are you sure? Kaplan thought I was dead after my accident. Maybe it wasn't Ted…?"

My dad sat at the foot of the bed, looking weary. "No. It was Ted. The firemen got to him too late. He's gone."

My mind reeled. After all that had happened to me…and now Ted…I couldn't believe my ears. I'd just seen my friend…and now he was gone forever…and there were so many questions I still wanted to ask him about the accident, like why he was going so fast that night, why the need to be in such a hurry…but now I would never get the chance. And I wanted to catch up on news about girls, sports, parties…and where he was working now. I'd heard he'd gotten fired from Mario's. In fact, I'd heard a lot of things through the grapevine, that Ted had become quieter since my accident, more cut off from people, almost a recluse.

"I just can't believe this…I was with him only hours ago. And he promised me he'd come over today. I was going to show him the exercise room you made me in the basement. He seemed really excited and supportive…." I trailed off. My dad stood up and moved to the head of my bed. He reached down and squeezed my shoulder.

"Ted's at peace now. He was always worried about you. He felt really bad about everything." He stared out the window a moment, where the sun was shining brightly through the leaves, then turned back to me. "Just remember the good times you had with him. That's all we can do."

For the next part of this story I must piece things together about Ted and the fire from articles and word of mouth. I was in such a state of shock over his loss that it took me a long time to accept he was gone. I chose not to read the paper at the time or go to the funeral. I had to get back to rehab the next day and continue my treatment for the following two weeks before I could be discharged. I was at the crossroads we all come to in our lives, and I had to choose to focus on getting better. I strongly believe that if I had dwelled at that time on the loss of my friend, I would have fallen into an irreversible depression.

During those last two weeks at Gaylord and in the months to come, I sensed Ted was pulling for me spiritually and pointing me in the direction of health. Whenever I would exercise, I would picture him smiling and giving me a thumbs up. And that is how I always will remember him.

I never learned exactly what happened to Ted. I only heard details here and there about the fire from others. When Ted got home that night, he wanted to have a steak sandwich. He would always grab a bite to eat before he went to bed. He put the steak in a pan and turned on the burner. Then he went upstairs to the third floor to his bedroom. In the meantime, he must have downed a beer and dozed off. Maybe he was tired from the stress of the day or so shocked from seeing me the way I had become from the accident—the shell of the person I used to be—that he just shut down and went to sleep.

I've come to understand that a grease fire started. It was an old house, and it went up like dry kindling. The fire spread fast, leaping up the kitchen curtains, and before long, the whole house was engulfed in flames. I hear his stepmother and little sister were rescued by firemen from the second-floor window. They weren't sure if Ted was home because his motorcycle was not in the driveway. He'd been dropped off by friends that night and left his motorcycle at Dave's house. His father was away on business.

The firemen wanted to be thorough, so they climbed up to the third floor, but they couldn't get in. They could see a light on in his room and the shadow of his body slumped against the door. One fireman fell through the roof three times trying to get to him. He finally made it to the door, but he had trouble pushing it open because Ted's body was blocking it. By the time he forced it open, Ted was gone. The smoke had asphyxiated him, and he was so dehydrated he was blown up like a balloon. The room was so hot a lightbulb melted. Those are the only details I know, but they sure stuck in my mind for a lifetime. I imagine he was buried next to his mother. I hope he's finally found peace.

After his death, his dad would often stop by to see how I was recovering. He would talk more to my father than me. I actually never had much of a conversation with him. He hid his loss well. They'd always talk outside in the yard, but I'd be so busy walking slow circles around the house that I didn't really hear what they said.

On my last day at Gaylord, I put on my street clothes and slicked my hair back. I was ready to take on the world. Sandy entered with a wheelchair.

"Looking sharp!" she said.

I turned to her, putting my comb away, "I'm ready to rock and roll. Can we stop on the way out? I want to say goodbye to Dave and wish him luck—the guy I gave the monkey to."

She nodded, "Great idea. I'm sure he will appreciate it."

It was an amazing feeling as she pushed me out of my room and down the long corridor to freedom. "You know, Mike, you've recovered faster than most patients who come through here. You should be very proud of yourself. To be honest, what you did is nothing short of a miracle."

"Thanks—I just want to get back to playing baseball again....and living a normal life. I'm gonna shoot for the sun!" She started to slow as we approached Dave's door. "It's not enough to just have potential. My coach used to say—potential is a nine-letter word, and it sits on the bench. You have to produce! And I guarantee you, Sandy, I *will* produce. You can bank on it!"

"From what you've done here—I *know* you will."

She turned and wheeled me into Dave's room. The moment I entered, he looked up from his crossword puzzle with a big smile.

"Congrats—I heard you're leaving?"

"Yeah, today's my big day. I see you got my friend watching over you." I nodded toward the monkey, which was sitting on his bedside table staring at us.

"Yeah, he's brought me some good luck already. Works like a charm."

"Be sure to pass him on when the time comes. And it will come before you know it." He stared at me, trying to absorb this thought—that maybe the light would appear sooner at the end of the tunnel.

"Before I know it..." he repeated, unconvinced.

"I'm living proof, Dave! The doctors never thought I'd walk again. Or do anything. But I always look to the future and picture myself accomplishing the impossible—like leaving this hospital and living my life again. You have to keep a positive train of thought all the time.

And give yourself goals. I can't tell you how many times I lay awake, remembering what it felt like to strum a guitar or push the lawnmower across the yard—things I once took for granted. What I'm saying is—shoot for the sun—Dave. That's what I do. I aim high."

He nodded, and a slow smile spread across his face. "Thanks, Mike."

"Well, I can't stay. Got people to see, places to go, dreams to catch! Take care!"

And with that I was whisked out, and twenty minutes later climbed all by myself into the passenger side of my Uncle Joe's Cadillac. Sandy shut the door and blew me a kiss through the window, and I was on my way, winding down the road, Gaylord finally and forever at my back.

We turned onto the Merritt and headed straight for home. Uncle Joe drove ten miles below the speed limit, as if I was fragile cargo, while my dad and Maryann sat in the backseat urging him to speed up.

"Come on, Uncle Joe, I want to get home!" I pleaded. I loved sitting in the place of honor up front—with plenty of legroom. He finally picked up the pace much to the relief of the growing line of cars behind us. "Well, I finally cleared that hurdle—no more Gaylord for me!" I looked in the rearview mirror and saw my dad crack a big smile. Maryann's eyes were glowing. "I'm ready for your training plan, Coach," I turned and smiled back at my dad.

He leaned forward and gave my shoulder a happy squeeze. "I'm ready for you."

CHAPTER TWENTY-THREE

That first week home my friends came to visit. I sat in my favorite armchair near the window. I had my leg braces on, but I never used my wheelchair in the house. I preferred to crawl around to make my body stronger. In order to teach myself to walk again, I knew I had to start at the beginning, like a child, but I was determined.

My friends gathered around me: Dave, Barrett, Jim, Brian, Susan, and Nicole. My mom served them fruit punch and homemade cookies, but everyone was in a quiet mood because we'd lost Ted only three weeks prior. I felt bad that I missed his funeral but knew at the same time that he would have understood. I looked around at all the somber faces. I wanted to say something to cheer them up, so I made this statement: "You see this cane right here?" I held it up boldly. Everyone's eyes were on me now. I pointed with it toward the window. "You see that maple out there. I promise you that I will hang this cane on that tree by Christmas."

There were smiles and looks of surprise all around.

Barrett gave me a thumbs up: "If anyone can do it, it's you!"

Susan shot me one of her megawatt smiles: "Go for it, Big One!"

I realized my dad had been standing in the kitchen archway listening. He smiled, too.

Then he said, "Hey, before you kids leave, you want to all come down and see Mike's new exercise room?"

Everyone stood up politely. My dad came over and helped support me by my left arm. I pushed myself up and used my right hand to grab hold of the cane. From the moment I got back from Gaylord, I told my dad, "Fold up that wheelchair and put it on the porch." He did just that, and I never touched it again.

My father guided me to the top of the basement stairs. My friends followed behind, then watched as I made my way, one step at a time, holding onto both rails, all the way down to the bottom. Only a few short months ago, that act would have been impossible.

A few minutes later, we were all downstairs taking a tour of my father's exercise masterpiece—a creation he'd been working on for weeks. He'd gone to great lengths to rig up my own home gym, specifically designed to retrain and strengthen my entire body to do everything it used to—and then some. There was a bench press for lifting weights, and the rowing machine my sister received from the New Canaan YMCA. He'd repaired the broken oar so expertly it looked shiny and brand new. He'd also set up a stationary bike and parallel bars, which not only provided a sense of security as I practiced walking, but also enabled me to putt golf balls into a can. My dad said this would help me gain back my coordination and ability to multitask physical actions. If I lost my balance while trying to putt them, I could just grab onto the bars. This was his way of building back my confidence, along with a sense of fun and optimism that I'd lost as a result of the severity of my accident. In the last few days, I'd already spent time down there acquainting myself with all of the equipment and exercises my dad developed for me.

The team at Gaylord, from doctors to therapists, was very impressed with my father. All that time I spent in the hospital, he'd devoted himself to studying books on rehabilitation—mind, body, and soul—and how they all interacted in the proper functioning of a healthy body. His readings ranged from complex medical journals to exercise books and spiritual texts. He spent many hours discussing my treatment and progress with doctors and therapists, making him a member of my recovery team.

Dr. Mulford, the one in charge of my case, often remarked that he would love to have my father work in the hospital helping other patients recover. And now I could really feel the results from even a few days down in the basement using the circuit he created. My arms and legs were getting stronger. My coordination was already starting to return. I felt a little less stiff and was even logging five miles per day on the bike. Everyone looked around and said things like, "Wow, Mike will be back in no time," and "Hey, Mr. Krysiuk, this place is really great! You should become a professional personal trainer—'cause you got everything covered here."

"Nah, I'm just here working with Mike. That's as far as I'm going as a personal trainer." But he smiled at them.

After my friends left, I felt pretty tired and told my dad I was going to rest for a while. I crawled down the hall to my bedroom, then pushed myself up onto the bed. I sat there a moment, caught my breath, then bent down to remove my shoe braces. As I pulled off the velcro and untied the shoes, I paused a moment, staring up at all the trophies on my shelf I'd acquired over the years. They caught the late afternoon light, gold and silver figurines holding baseball bats or leaping up to slam dunk a ball. There was even a Cub Scouts soap box derby car—a first place win when I was twelve. For a minute I felt a wave of nostalgia mixed with intense sadness. But I immediately pushed it aside and made a decision never to feel like that again—ever—about my future. I was always going to be Mr. Positive from now on. If I couldn't achieve a goal today, then I would try tomorrow, until I finally succeeded. *Starting right now,* I told myself firmly, *you will recover 110 percent from this accident and succeed in your life's ambition, whatever that may be!*

My sister popped her head in at that exact moment, interrupting my psychological cheerleading—rooting myself to success.

"Hey, Mike," she said in a bright voice, "I've set up tutoring for you to finish up those classes you need to graduate. It starts in two weeks. Mr. Georges is coming over for physics, Mr. Savago for math, Mr. Fox for electronics, and Mr. Arbolino for economics."

"Thank God it's not Kaplan!"

She laughed. "You've had enough trauma."

"Bring in the clowns! I'm ready!"

After that day my friends never came back to visit, but they did slow their cars if they saw me out in the yard exercising and would give me a quick "Hi" out the window. It was hard not being part of the click anymore. For a long time I lost connection with my peers and the world. My cousins, at least, came over and played Gin Rummy with me or watched sports, but that was the extent of my interaction with kids my own age.

I don't blame these friends that I once spent so much time with. I changed. And they changed, too. This accident turned me into a person they did not recognize anymore. I was playing on a different ball field with a different game plan. I not only had to teach my body how to move again, but I also had to learn how to speak clearly, laugh, and even cry.

My mind still knew how to do everything, but the wires of communication were tangled. Rewiring my brain to do simple tasks seemed monumental. I am sure that even just the slurring of my words caused my friends to feel uncomfortable, and this I don't blame them for. My dad saw the issue and developed a technique for fixing it. He recorded me reading out loud and then played back the tape so I could hear exactly where I needed to improve. I didn't always like this process because hearing the way I spoke was very frustrating, even humiliating. But over time, I began to speak more clearly and get my thoughts out faster.

Unfortunately, my friends were not there to see and hear my improvements, but nothing was going to stop me from pushing for recovery. There were times I stood at the living room window and watched the world go by: neighbors heading to work or home in their cars, walking dogs, pushing babies in strollers, the paperboy shoving the world's news into our mailboxes, my friends whizzing by on motorcycles, even the birds winging from tree to tree or squirrels jumping from branch to branch created patterns for my eyes to entertain me. There was life out there—and I wanted to be part of it again.

In the afternoons, my tutors would stop by. My mom always greeted them with a smile. She made everyone feel at home, providing a cup of coffee or the exact type of tea someone preferred. Or she would offer them one of her famous cold glasses of fruit punch concocted by mixing different juices and iced teas together—people loved that! The house always smelled of something good cooking on the stove. Even though I lost my sense of smell from the accident, I knew her food enticed everyone due to the comments my teachers made.

"What's that you got cooking there, Mrs. Krysiuk? Smells amazing."

"Oh, just a leg of lamb with my secret seasonings."

While I worked at the card table in the living room, she would labor over the stove, stirring a pot of stew, or pulling some casserole from the oven. Mom was always dressed beautifully in her signature style, a crisp white blouse with a pretty pin and tailored pants, her hair reminiscent of her heyday in the 1940s. Even if she'd just come in from gardening, one of her favorite pastimes, her blouse remained immaculate, and her hair perfectly pinned in place. That was one of her gifts—always giving off a sense of order and peace, making everyone feel welcome and well taken care of in the Krysiuk household.

In fact, when my father used to come home from work, in those days before my accident, she would greet him, freshly showered and dressed in something extra nice, putting away the work clothes of the day. She even put on her favorite lipstick. This was her way of always making him feel special, and their relationship was very close. The romance was never lost between them, it only deepened over the years, and no matter what they went through, they stayed bonded, partners that faced the world and its troubles together.

And one of those troubles, small as it may seem compared to my accident, was getting all my work done so I could graduate. My classmates had already accomplished this and were heading off to college. I was now a semester behind, and though I was already accepted to Norwalk Tech, I needed to get that high school diploma under my belt. But the blow to my head made it hard for me to retain information.

Before the accident, I was a good student—second honors, which is B level. My strongest area was math. It came easily, and I often helped out my friends if they had a homework question. One of my favorite high school classes was electronics because, as a kid, I loved working with my dad in the basement, fixing old TVs and radios. I knew I wanted to eventually pursue this as a career. Norwalk Tech would be the perfect place for me, but now I had some new hurdles to overcome to get there and succeed.

My fear was not the work of retraining the mind—my memory was already coming back—but a fear of failure. If I didn't grasp something right away with my tutors, I was scared they would label me "handicapped," and that term might stick for life. I was NOT going to let that happen! I went to extreme lengths to pass everything. I spent hours and hours studying and reading out loud. I discovered if I spoke and heard myself, I could retain it a lot faster. Perhaps, this was related to my musical gift.

Though my guitar remained in the case for some time after that evening I tried to play it for Ted and the gang, I eventually decided to pick it up and return to daily practice. I had a chair in the middle of my bedroom with a music stand always open. I sat there whenever I wasn't exercising, trying to master the sheet music of my former playing days. But I couldn't get my fingers to do their old dance.

I wasn't about to let that stop me. I started to write my own songs, with the chords that came easiest, including new chords I created myself. I wrote lyrics, too—songs about my life, everything I'd been through, from trying to be popular to losing everything, to announcing my grand return to humanity—to civilization itself! That final piece, titled, "The Big One," became my theme song.

I had no idea when I first wrote it that, one day, I would be sitting in restaurants and bars playing it for a crowd, even having it requested many times. One of the greatest things about that song was its upbeat chorus, which inspired people to join in. The first time I ever played it for someone was for my sister. By then, I'd really gotten the flow back in my hands. I'd never lost my callouses, just my dexterity. Finally, my fingers were flying again.

Maryann poked her head in one day and said, "That sounds great! What are you playing?"

"It's called 'The Big One.'"

"Can I hear it from the top?"

I was born to perform, so I loved this moment. "Sure, take a seat!"

Maryann sat on my bed and looked at me expectantly. I strummed the G chord and began to sing from the top:

> *Every town has its legendary figure*
>
> *Or someone who everybody else is afraid of—*
>
> *LA has its one, New York has its one*
>
> *But Westport has THE BIG ONE...*

The song had a driving beat, and I could see Maryann tapping her foot. I knew I had a hit! By the time I reached the last chorus she was singing along with me:

> *The Big One*
>
> *Oh, The Big One's coming*
>
> *The Big One, The Big One*
>
> *Oh, The Big Bad One!*

I finished with a flourish and looked over at my sister. She was smiling and looked the happiest I'd seen her in a long time.

"Way to go, bro! You got a winner!"

CHAPTER TWENTY-FOUR

Over the next four months, September through December, I made giant strides in every part of my life. Imagine one of those montages you see in a film—I was always in motion, from the time I woke up to the moment I hit the pillow at night—working at the exercise machines, pushing a baby carriage filled with fifty-pound sandbags up and down the driveway, my father rooting me along at my side, or surrounded by scaffolding he took from work, so I could stand steady while shooting baskets. He caught all the rebounds from my errant shots, but I did make a few! Like I said—always shoot for the sun!

I also completed all my course work and received Bs across the board. Mr. King called my mother to say I was ready to graduate. I remember the moment she turned from the phone, tears stinging her eyes, and said, "You did it, Mike—you're graduating! And you're going to walk up to that podium and get your diploma. Now this is a nice Christmas present."

But I had one more big walk to complete before that. I needed to keep that promise to myself and hang my cane on the maple tree, even if my friends wouldn't be there to see it.

Since I'd been home, I'd progressed from two quad canes to one quad cane, to a single cane, and that was the object I would be hooking on the lower limb of the tree. As my mother hung up the phone, I moved to the window and looked out at the front yard.

The maple was bare and the sun illuminated every familiar branch. I watched a few flakes drift lazily down through the shining air, melting the moment they hit the grass. The time was right. I knew I needed to go now, while there was no snow on the ground, and make it straight to that tree.

I turned to my mom, "Go get Dad and Maryann—I have an early Christmas gift for all of you."

My mom shot me a confused look, "What do you mean, Mike?"

"Just get them and I'll show you."

A few minutes later, the Krysiuk team was assembled on the front steps. I smiled at my faithful trio—my constant source of inspiration and faith—the real reason I was standing here now. In his hurry my father had only thrown on his winter hat (no coat, just a sweatshirt), and my mom stood beside him still in her apron, one arm hooked happily through his. Maryann took a step down to the yard to get a better view. There was a feeling of expectancy in the air. "Watch this!" I said.

Taking a deep breath, I turned toward the tree. With slow, deliberate steps, I walked toward the trunk. The ground was rock solid from the cold, giving my cane the support I needed. I stopped before the trunk and stared at the spot where I had once carved my initials as a kid with a pocket knife. Then I lifted the cane like an Olympic torch, glanced at my family, then chasing away all those goblins of fear and failure, found my balance, and hooked the handle triumphantly over the lowest branch. I let go, watching it swing there for a moment, then took a few steps back and found my footing. I was standing solid on my own two feet. Finally, I was free!

I looked up through the forked branches to the winter sky. White flakes were falling harder now, drifting down between the dark boughs. In that moment, I knew I would never use that cane again.

I threw my arms up in victory and declared: "The Big One's back! And the sky's the limit!"

The moment those words left my lips, the snow began to fall in earnest, as if the very elements heard me. And what a beautiful sight it was—refreshing—miraculous—the flakes spinning down like mini stars between my fingertips to touch my upturned face.

"Alright!" My father shouted behind me, "I knew you could do it, Mike!"

And then my sister—"All that hard work paid off! You're a free man now!"

My mother's voice seemed lit with happiness: "Way to go, Big One! Way to go…."

With my hands still raised overhead, I pointed at the sky and proclaimed: "This is why I shoot for the sun, because even if you miss, you'll land among the stars and that…" I slowly swiveled to face them, feeling a surge of energy from head to toe as I spread my arms wide, as if to gather my faithful family into a huge and heartfelt embrace, "is a great place to be."

EPILOGUE

On a bright morning in September of 1975, I proudly pulled into the lot of Norwalk State Technical College. I was playing Led Zeppelin's "Whole Lot of Love" and feeling ready to start this new season of my life. I turned off the car and sat there a moment in silence, staring at all the students passing down the walkway toward the big double doors. I felt nervous, knowing I had to make new friends and acclimate, but I also realized that many of these kids were also there for the first time and probably felt the same way.

I grabbed my bookbag and maneuvered myself out of the car. My desert boots (a gift from my mom) hit the asphalt—no more metal braces for me! I stopped using them weeks ago—tossing them into the back of my closet. I would not need their assistance again. I stood up and shouldered my bag. I felt a sense of expectation and energy—it was going to be a great day, even though I knew there would be some hurdles ahead.

By the end of the first afternoon, I felt pumped about my classes but also realized I needed to refine my study habits—this was going to be an accelerated year of growth. It was easy making new friends, though, because we were all being thrown into this fishbowl together and, from the beginning, helped each other stay positive and focussed. The associates degree in electrical engineering we sought—all 120 of us—was a very challenging program. Two years later, upon graduation, only twenty-six of us remained.

The teachers were stern and always down to business. As each semester went by, more and more students dropped or failed out. I spent the majority of my free time studying and getting extra help when needed from my professors. They were always happy to assist me and respected my intense focus. Gone was my cavalier high school attitude. No more partying, trying to fit in, or chasing girls. I was grateful for the second chance to pursue my dreams and make the most of my time. There were six of us who had to take a summer course in advanced applied mathematics to graduate. This shifted my graduation schedule so I couldn't walk down the aisle and shake the dean's hand. My diploma came in the mail. I still recall slowly opening the envelope and pulling out that thick paper with the school seal. There was my name and the date of graduation, June 1977. I immediately framed it and hung it proudly in my bedroom above my sports trophies.

A few weeks later, I landed a job as an electrical technician at a Norwalk firm that built regulators for electric motors. I was a test technician, which meant that I had to sit at a work table seven hours a day, focussing on the complex operation of machinery, testing speeds, frequencies, and the compatibility of the regulator to the motor. I sat alone in a windowless office bent over the mechanism, exposed to high frequencies, and I began to develop severe headaches. This happened to other people too, but perhaps my head trauma made it worse. I often blacked out, waking up with my head on the table.

I discussed the issue with my family, and we all decided I should leave this dangerous job and pursue further education, shifting my major to accounting. The associates degree in engineering was now a feather in my cap; it taught me strong study habits and built my confidence back. Now it was time to pursue a bachelors in accounting. and to that end I applied to the University of Bridgeport and soon found myself sitting in the classroom again, focusing on financial and marketing matters. I enjoyed the challenge and graduated with the dean's award for the college of business. I'll never forget walking confidently down the aisle, my family and friends cheering me on. When I received the award, the teacher made a small speech, noting my persistence and standard of excellence, skills first honed in the crucible of my accident.

Throughout the years I pursued higher education, I also continued to work on my music. It became my outlet from academics and stress. I had not only regained my flexibility but also expanded my repertoire, and I was writing lots of songs, enough to make a few albums. But what's the point of always playing alone in a room? I wanted to expand my horizons, and I loved to perform. I could not use sports any longer as my public arena, so I changed my focus to music and the arts.

One day, almost on a whim, I decided to go to an open mic night at a small pub in Westport called Grass Roots. It was a quaint little dive of a place with a small stage. They served wine, cheese, and sandwiches, and the crowd was always enthusiastic. I was around twenty-three when I first stepped through the doors, my guitar in hand. I signed my name to the sheet and waited my turn with no fear, only excitement.

When it was my turn to play, I pulled my acoustic out and walked up to the stool. I turned to face the local crowd. My mom and dad had shown up, my sister, too. When the host asked my name, I smiled at all those faces, and suddenly found myself saying, "Ziggy Rainbow!" It was a spur of the moment creation, but it has stuck with me to this day. I played a few popular songs, such as "I'm Easy," by Keith Carradine and "Knocking on Heaven's Door," by Bob Dylan, followed up with two of my own creations, "I've Changed My Style," and my closing song with its rousing chorus, "The Big One."

The first original piece was a reflection upon my life. I told the story of growing up from an innocent small town boy to a mature and wiser man. The last song, "The Big One," seemed to be the most popular, inspiring people to join the chorus, and I felt jubilant when their voices filled the room.

After that first successful night at Grass Roots, I made sure to come back. I also began to play my electric at the Tin Whistle (a larger local venue) to packed houses. The last night I played at the Tin Whistle, I heard the next morning that it burned down. Fortunately, there were no casualties, but now there were fewer places to play. So I put my guitar back in its case and decided to pursue acting.

Growing up, my focus was always sports. I'd never participated in any local theatre productions, but now in my twenties, I decided to pursue stand up comedy. It brought together my love of acting with my gift of humor that had been so necessary during my medical struggles. I signed up for a class in stand-up and discovered it not only made me feel useful, but I had a real knack for it. It was a total thrill to perform in local comedy clubs and even once on a New York City stage. I never used the accident as a source of material for my routines. I found nothing funny in what happened to me. Instead, I focussed my comedy around my height, dating, and playing sports. The positive response to my comedy schtick sparked me to pursue auditions for stage and film.

I signed up for local acting classes and then went to study at the Actors Studio in New York City. My confidence grew in the areas of acting choices and audience interaction. I became more natural on stage, making my characters more believable. The exercises also helped with physical movement and a stronger stage presence. After a year of training, I started to audition and land roles at local theaters. My favorite part was big Jule in *Guys and Dolls*. Everything about this performance came naturally to me, from Jules' accent to his physical movements; I knew how to embody an intimidating hustler that never gives up.

After *Guys and Dolls,* I set my sights on television and motion pictures. After a few auditions I was cast in a TV pilot playing a mafia hitman at a dance club. The pilot never made the air, but it inspired a TV cop show that ran for two or three seasons and then was canceled. I went to a few more auditions in NYC but had no luck. I was often told that I had a great audition but I was too tall and would not fit into the cast. Not long after these rejections I suddenly landed a part in a motion picture starring Leonardo DiCaprio, "Revolutionary Road." I played a disgruntled audience member who stands up and throws his hands in the air, then exits the room. It took around ten takes to satisfy the director, but finally he said, "Perfect Big Guy—you got it!"

The confidence I was gaining from my fledgling acting career was spilling over into my personal life. I hadn't dated much since the accident, but I decided to engage the services of a local matchmaking company and it wasn't long before I met the woman I would eventually marry. We hit it off from the first date, and a year later we were married in a local church. I am the proud father of two lovely daughters. I love them dearly, and they will always be my buddies. After seven years, things didn't work out in the marriage, and my wife and I grew apart. As a result, we got a divorce.

I then wrote a small book about the car accident titled, "Why Me, Why Now?" It described the coma in detail and my journey to recovery. I self-published it and gave it to friends and family. I was invited to give a talk on the book at the Westport Library and also to speak to young people at schools. A few years later, I co-authored a play about that terrible accident. It was called "I Don't See My Shadow." The original work was performed at the Westport Historical Society to a full house.

My show received a standing ovation that lasted five minutes. Cooper Ramsey, the talented young actor who played me, left not a dry eye in the house. I gave a small talk after the show, answering questions and explaining the fuller context of my story.

While I was following my dreams in the arts, I met and married my soulmate, Lori, my true love—she even laughs at my jokes! She encourages me in all my dreams and shares my vision for seeing my story on the silver screen.

I've been working on getting my message out for years, using myself as an example of what the wrong choices can and most certainly will do to your life. I hope that by reading *The Big One* you have seen what happens when a person walks in other peoples' shadows, whether that be me, you, your friends, anybody, and everybody. That is why I live by this golden rule, as shown to me in my coma at the crossroads of my life: Shoot for the sun in everything you do, because even if you miss, you will land among the stars, and that is a great place to be.

Follow your dreams—they do come true. I am living proof!

Mike's christening, March 1957, 3 months old; Maryann, 11 years old

Mike – 1 year old, January 1958

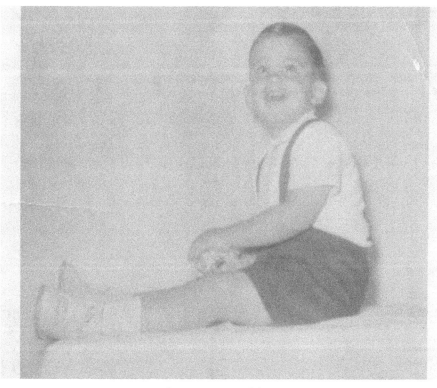

Mike – 3 years old, 1960

The neighborhood gang – Easter Sunday 1962 – left to right: Mike, Cousin Johnny, Cousin Nancy, Cousin Richard, brothers Steve (friend) and Dave (friend, one of Ted's gang)

Mike and Maryann – October 1965, 8 years old, 19 years old,
New York World's Fair

Mike – 9 years old, August 1966 - fielding

Mike – 9 years old, August 1966 – hitting

Westport Little League "Yankees" 1966, Coach, Frank; Manager, (Uncle) Joe; Mike is second from right in back row. Mike is 9 years old and taller than the 12-year-olds.

Mike's 6th grade class, 1968. Mike is on the far right in the last row in the white turtleneck.

Frank and Anne, 51 years old; Maryann 22 years old; Mike, 11 years old, January 1968

Frank and Anne, 51 years old, January 1968

Frank in full WWII uniform, undated photo

Frank in drill uniform at Wheeler, 1944

Frank with rifle in sitting position at Wheeler, 1943 or 1944

Frank and Anne at home, 8 Oak Ridge Park, 1975

Frank, Anne, and Maryann, 1987 – The Krysiuk Team

Mike, post-accident, at Maryann's house, undated photo

Mike and Anne, undated photo

Frank and Mike at a wedding, undated photo

Frank, Mike, and Maryann, undated photo

Frank in the vegetable garden, undated photo

Frank caught a big one (striped bass), undated photo

The house that Frank built, undated photo

Frank and Anne, undated photo

Frank and Anne, still dancing, at a wedding, undated photo

Mike, 2015